Postharvest Management of Fruit Crops

The Authors

Professor (Dr.) Kaushal Kumar Misra received his Ph.D. Horticulture degree in the year 1986 from Govind Ballabh Pant University of Agriculture and Technology, Pantnagar, U.K. He did his post doctorate degree from V. P. I. and State University, Blacksburg, Virginia, U.S.A. during 1989. He started his career as Senior Research Assistant on June 08, 1974 from Pantnagar. He was selected as Junior Research Officer, Horticulture on April 1, 1978. He was selected as Senior Research Officer/Associate Professor, Horticulture on April 1, 1991. Dr. Misra was selected as Professor, Horticulture on July 27, 1998. He was Officer Incharge at Research Station, Sui, Lohaghat District Pithoragarh, U.P. from January 12, 1992 to March 31, 1994, then again as Associate Director/Joint Director at H.R.C., Patharchatta from November 19, 1997 to July 15, 1999. He was selected as Head of Department of Horticulture from November 1, 2004 to December 18, 2005 and September 30, 2006 to June 01, 2009. He published 35 books, 207 research papers, 14 review papers, 150 popular articles and more than dozen of book chapters in review books to his credits. He was awarded Dr. Rajendra Prasad Puruskar, 1984 from I.C.A.R., New Delhi, awarded by Man of Year 1997-1999 by ABI, North Carolina (U.S.A.), conferred, ISHRD Fellowship in September, 2004 from Indian Society of Horticultural Research and Development, Uttarakhand, Best Citizen of India Awards, 2006 and 2010, New Delhi and fellowship from Horticultural Society of India award, 2013. Seventeen Ph.D. and fourteen M.Sc. (Ag.) Horticulture students received his/her degree under his guidance. He has got 44 years of experience of teaching, research and extension education.

Postharvest Management of Fruit Crops

— *Authors* —

Dr. Kaushal Kumar Misra

Ph.D., P.D. (U.S.A.),
Professor and Former Head

Department of Horticulture, College of Agriculture,
Govind Ballabh Pant University of Agriculture and Technology,
Pantnagar – 263 145, District – Udham Singh Nagar,
Uttarakhand India

BIOTECH

2020

BIOTECH BOOKS®

ISBN 978-81-7622-437-6

Published by: **BIOTECH BOOKS®**
4762-63/23, Ansari Road, Darya Ganj,
New Delhi - 110 002
Phone: 09899295259
E-mail: biotechbooks@yahoo.co.in

Typeset at: **Classic Computer Services**
Delhi - 110 035

Printed at: **Replika Press Pvt. Ltd.**

PRINTED IN INDIA

Dedicated To

My Father-in-Law

Shri Yadunandan Prasad Agnihotri

Who has great love to horticulture

Preface

Management of postharvest fruit crops are written in postharvest handling and management of fruits. Postharvest managements of fruit crops are 13 chapters. The first chapter includes judging maturity of fruits. The second chapter includes harvesting and packing of fruits. The third chapter includes varietal suitability for processing. The fourth chapter deals with storage of fruits. The fifth chapter deals with postharvest handling. The sixth chapter deals with postharvest classification of fruits. The seventh chapter deals with process of maturity and maturity standards. The eighth chapter deals with biochemical changes during fruit ripening. The nineth chapter deals with ethylene management in fruits. The tenth chapter deals with controlled atmosphere storage. The eleventh chapter deals with chemical changes during ripening and senescence. The twelveth chapter deals with regulation of ripening and senescence. The thirteenth chapter deals with postharvest handling of mango fruits. The glossary containing related terms have been given. The selected references presented at the end can be useful to obtain for further information.

The efforts have been made to describe various chapters of postharvest management of fruit crops in a systematic and comprehensive manner. The subject matter was illustrated with tables and figures wherever felt necessary. The book has been written keeping in view the requirements of the graduate students, scientists, teachers and workers in the postharvest management of fruit crops. All the suggestions for further improvement of the book will be highly appreciated. The author is grateful to their several students who assisted them in their scientific pursuit in postharvest management of fruit crops during the last four decades at Govind Ballabh Pant University of Agriculture and Technology, Pantnagar, Uttarakhand, India. The author is thankful to his wife Mrs. Manjul Mishra and daughter Mrs. Kanan Kaushal for assisting in many ways. Thanks are due to first author's sons Mr. Praduman Kaushal, Mr. Piyush Kaushal, Mr. Panini Kaushal, son-in-law Mr. Satyajeet Pandey, dauthers-in-law Mrs. Pratibha Kaushal, Mrs.

Subhi Kaushal, Mrs. Neha Kaushal, grandsons Mr. Pratham Kumar, Mr. Prayan Kaushal and granddaughter Ms. Aadiya Kaushal and Ms. Saanvi Kaushal. Thanks are also due to Mr. Shailendra Kumar, Head Assistant for typing the manuscript.

Dr. Kaushal Kumar Misra

Contents

Chapter 1

Judging Maturity of Fruits

A fruit is a living and respiring edible tissue. Development starts with the formation of the edible part such as the setting of a fruit, the emergence of a seedling, the swelling of a root, tuber or bulb or the elongation of a stalk or petiole. Development occurs largely before harvest and includes prematuration and part of maturation. The maturation in fruits reach when the edible portion has attained some desirable conditions. Harvest is a single deliberate action to separate the food stuff from its growth medium and all the succeeding actions are defined as postharvest actions. Ripening marks the completion of development and the commencement of senescence. Time of harvest of a fruit is a complicated problem as great differences occur in the rate of development and maturation. In many fruit species blossoming and fertilization occur over a relatively short period while in others production of blossoms continue over an extended period. Fruits developing at such different times within a tree or bush or in the orchard or garden may well be affected by differing endogenous and environmental factors.

The stage and mature of physiological development play an important role in developing, handling and storage strategies. Successful marketing of fresh commodity requires the selection of proper mature fruits at harvest. Even though immature fruits can soften, the time required for softening is much longer than mature ones and the fruit will not develop the desirable flavour and texture identifiable with mature fruits. In addition, increased incidence of fruit shriveling and decay are often characteristic of these fruits following harvest. The fruits harvested at late maturity stage, soften, very fast which is difficult to check under ordinary storage conditions and heavy losses may occur due to diseases and disorders. The development of physiological disorders during storage can be controlled, to a sometimes considerable extent by harvesting the fruits at the appropriate stage of maturity. The maturity in the fruit crops may be defined as the stage of development, when a plant or plant part possesses the prerequisites for utilization by consumers for a particular purpose. It may be determined by (i) visual means like size, colour, shoulder growth and so on (ii) physical means like firmness, specific gravity (iii) computation as days after fruit set or growth and heat units (iv) physiological methods like respiration and (v) chemical methods like TSS, acid, vitamins and starch. To assess the maturity of fruit on anyone harvest index may employ certain limitations as during the growth there are number of factors like nutritional status of soil, weather conditions, sowing time, cultural practices used affect them adversely or favourably. Keeping in view the limitations it is possible to combine some of the above mentioned indices of maturity to assess the harvest stage. The harvest maturity of some of the fruits is discussed below:

Apple

The maturity of fruit in apple is generally assessed on the basis of number of days of fruit growth, heat units, flesh firmness and the contents of soluble solids, starch and ethylene. The number of days from full blook to harvest is the most reliable guide to maturity which vary among cultivars. The harvest of delicious apples may be divided into following three phases.

i. Marly maturity, 135-140 days from full bloom.
ii. Optimum maturity, 140-150 days from full bloom.
iii. Late maturity, more than 150 days.

Banana

It is harvested green at varying stages of maturity depending upon the destination, for long distance transport 75-80 per cent mature and for short distance transport 90-100 per cent mature fruits are harvested. The maturity indices generally used in India are peel to pulp ratio (1:2), days of emergence of inflorescence, disappearance of angularity of the fingers, drying of leaves and brittleness of the floral ends. To determine the proper time of harvesting it is best to supplement 'fullness of finger' with size and the number of days it takes from emergence to maturity. Dwarf Cavendish takes 100-120 days while Robusta takes 130-140 days after shooting. It takes about 12 to 15 months for Cavendish cultivars and 15 to 18 months for Poovan, Monthan and others after planting to be ready for harvest.

Citrus

There are lot of differences in maturity indices in different citrus varieties but most useful criterion to assess maturity are colour break and soluble solids to acid ratio of the fruit pulp. In India, citrus fruits are generally harvested between December to February when rind colour changes from green to orange, acidity is reached around 0.4 per cent and TSS is between 12 to 14 per cent. However, the maturity indices are different in case of sweet oranges and they are harvested when rind colour changes to yellow. The acidity of juice is around 0.3 per cent and TSS is 12 per cent.

Guava

In India, two crops of guava are obtained in a year, one in the rainy season and the other in winter season. Fruits of winter season crop are better in quality with less decay loss as compared to those of rainy season crop. The storage life of fruits of winter season crop is better. In guavas, the maturity indices may vary according to season and variety. Specific gravity of fruits has been found to be the best index for harvesting. At maturity guava fruits should have specific gravity around 1.0 wit skin colour changing towards yellow. For long distance transport, guava fruits having specific gravity around 1.02 will be better to harvest. However, other characters like TSS, acidity and vitamin C have also been well correlated but these vary according to variety, area and harvesting season.

Table 1: Fruit Harvest Maturities

Crops	*Characters*
Apple	Growth period, Flesh firmness TSS, Starch content.
Banana	Growth period, Diameter, Angularity, Flesh firmness, Peel to Pulp ratio.
Citrus	Juice content, TSS, Acid, TSS to Acid ratio.
Grape	TSS, Acidity, TSS to Acid ratio.
Guava	Colour break, Specific gravity.
Mango	Surface and Flesh colour, Growth period, TSS, TSS to Acid ratio.
Papaya	Growth period, Colour break, Sugars.
Peach	Colour change.
Pear	Surface colour, Growth period, Flesh firmness.
Pineapple	Extent of eye development, Colour change, TSS.
Plum	Growth period, Flesh firmness, TSS, TSS to Acid ratio.
Sapota	Colour change, Brown scaly external material shedding.
Karonda	Colour changes from pink to brown.
Bael	Colour changes from green to yellow.

Mango

The determination of maturity in mangoes has been tried on the basis of external colour, shoulder growth, shape and size. However, these characters were not found suitable for all the varieties of the fruit. The period of growth from fruit set and heat units have been well correlated to maturity. Whereas specific gravity more than 1.0 was not found suitable in all the cultivars. It is reported that mango fruit takes 12 to 16 weeks from fruit set to harvest maturity depending on the cultivar. The maturity in Alphanso mango reaches around 16 weeks of fruit growth when specific gravity of fruit is more than 1.0. In most of the cultivars like, Dashehari, Baneshan, Bangalora, the period of fruit growth was found to be more reliable maturity index than specific gravity as most of the fruit at the time of harvesting were floaters. The chemical composition like TSS, TSS:acid ratio, starch and carotenoids are also found to be well correlated with harvest maturity. Respiration climacteric has also been used to assess maturity in some cultivars.

Papaya

Under optimum conditions, the growth and development of papaya proceed at a faster rate. Seeds germinate in two weeks, flowers and fruits are produced in the leaf axils after a juvenile period. In about 5 months from transplanting, the seedlings flower and set fruit. Depending on the climate, fruits mature within 4 to 6 months. Fruits showing streaks of yellow colour are harvested. Generally, the harvesting of ripe fruits start in about 9-10 months from the time the seedlings are transplanted in the field.

Chapter 2

Harvesting and Packing of Fruits

Proper care in harvesting and packing are essential to presume subsequent postharvest quality of fruits and to reduce spoilage during storage. Faculty harvesting and rough packing affects storability of fruit produce. On storage, bruises and injuries appear first as brown spots which turned blackish, making the commudity unattractive and impaired the marketability of produce. This is because of biological oxidation of phenolic compounds, present in the peel. Injuries to the peel or stalk-end serve as avenue for microorganisms and lead to rotting. Moreover, rate of repiration (storage index) and endogenous ethylene (ripening harmone) production increases markedly by the damages causes early onset of senescence and thus reducing the storage life of the fruit produce.

Method of Harvesting

Method of harvesting vary according to the crop and region. Generally, different kinds of fruits require different methods of harvesting. Some fruits such as guava, mango and citrus may easily be plucked by pulling though there is always a possibility of tearing-off a piece of flesh or skin. The harvesting is also done with the aid of clipper or shear. Fruits born on high branches create a problem during harvesting. Commonly, a long pole attached with a plastic or rope net bag is used in picking the fruits. The fruits may be harvested mechanically or chemically using higher dose of ethephon. Recently, K.K.V. Dapoli has fabricated harvester popularly known as Dapoli harvester. The method of harvesting of certain commercial horticultural crops are as below:

(1) Mango

Generally, the fruits are harvested by hand or by snapping or clipping the peduncle (8-10 mm) at the base, fruits not reached by hands are most often retrieved with poles adopted with a cutting blade or bag. The harvesting is usually done in the early hours of morning and are heaped under a shade to avoid the building-up of field heat.

(2) Guava

Guava is hand picked 2-3 times a week during 8 to 10 week harvest period. Sometimes, guava fruits are harvested with stalk alongwith foliage. Such harvested fruits can be kept longer under ambient conditions if packed in polyethylene bags. The storability can be further extended if such fruits are stored at 5-7°C in cold storage.

(3) Banana

Commercially, bananas are harvested green at varying stages of maturity, when they are to be transported to distant places. Nature banana is harvested with s sickle. The bunch should not fall to the ground but hang-on to avoid injury. The bunch is held and its peduncle is severed. About 30 cm. of the stalk is left to make handling easy. The hands are separated for easy and tight packing.

(4) Citrus

Harvesting of mature citrus is done either by pulling the fruit or clipping it from the tree. Pulling is faster and prevents long term. The fruit is twisted at an angle to the twig and jerked downwards, to detach. Loose skinned oranges are likely to be torn-off easily if pulled with the hand. If clipped, a shear or clipper is used. A short, slightly curved blunt shear is best suited for this purpose. The peduncle should be short, otherwise if it is long, it will be in-convenient during packaging and may cause mechanical injury during transportation.

Packaging

Packaging of fresh produce has been practiced since man first began to trade in these commodities. The two main functions of packaging are, to assemble the produce in convenient units for handling and to protect the produce during transportation, storage and marketing operations. The earliest packages were mostly constructed of plant materials such as woven leaves, reeds and grass stems and were designed to be carried by man. Later beasts of burden were used and the size of packages increased. Today, in developing countries like India, produce is transported and sold in a wide range of packages constructed of wood, fibre board, jute (hassion), or plastics. Current methods are often wasteful of raw materials as most packages are not reused. Thus, common packages are, wooden boxes, wire bound boxes, baskets made of bamboo, Cajanua or mulberry of different shapes like conical, cylindrical, telescopic and modified rectangular in shape, corrugated fibre board boxes, plastic containers, jute (hassion) bags are under practice. Beside this, certain packaging materials like newspaper, tissue paper, soft dry hays, paddy straw, wood dust green leaves and egg trays are commonly used to avoid bruising during transportation, marketing and storage of fruit produce.

Modern packaging for fresh produce is expected to meet a wide range of requirements which may be briefed as follows:

1. The packages must have sufficient mechanical strength to protect the contents during handling, transport and stacking.
2. The material of construction must not contain chemical which could transfer to the produce and be toxic to it or to man.
3. The package must meet handling and marketing requirements in terms of weight, size and shape.
4. The packages should allow rapid cooling of the contents. Furthermore, the permeability of plastic films to respiratory gases might also be important.
5. The mechanical strength should largely be unaffected by its moisture content when wet or at high humidities. The package might be required to exclude water from the produce or to prevent dehydration of the produce.
6. The security of the package or its case of opening and closing might be important in some marketing situations.
7. The cost of the package in relation to the value and the required extent of protection of the contents should be as low as possible.

Effect of Packaging in Produces Quality

Fruits vary widely in their susceptibility to mechanical damage. The choice of package and packing method must take account of different causes of mechanical injury to produce such as cuts, compressions, impacts and vibrations. Impact bruising is caused by sudden application of force, for example dropping of packages or impact shocks during handling and transport. Vibration, common during transport, causes abrasion ranging from light rub marks to removal off, not only skin but also some of the flesh. In the damaged tissues of the commodity all these injuries turn brown through oxidation of tannins and exposure of similar materials to air. Thus, the produce is disfigured and its market value is reduced. Furthermore, these injuries are avenues for infection and increased respiration. Hence, the rate of deterioration increases which caused immediate loss of edible material.

Two important principles should be considered at the time of packaging: (1) Individual specimens should not move with respect to each other or the walls of the packages to avoid vibration injury and (ii) the packages should be full without over filling or packing too tightly which increases compression and impact bruising. Thus, the individual items must be held firmly but not too tightly, within the package. In this respect, packaging can be made more protective by individual wrapping each piece of produce or be isolating each piece as in the cell pack and the tray pack methods for fruits.

Mechanical Strength of Package

Package must retain its mechanical strength throughout the marketing chain to avoid mechanical injury. Under conditions of high humidity, the package material must not absorb moisture. The widely used fibre-board cartons and trays rapidly lose strength as they absorb moisture and so they are less satisfactory in tropical conditions and in high humidity cool storage. They can, however, be protected if fully impregnated with wax or similar water proof material.

Paking and Storage

Package Dimensions

The dimensions of packages are important; the size and shape should provide economic use of materials, optimal strength and easy and secure handling, loading and stacking. The optimal length width ratio is about 1.5:1. With the advent of mechanical handling of groups of packages, there have been strong moves to standardize package sizes which make the best use of available space, stack well on standard pallets and so reduce costs.

The size of packages should be standardized to promote more efficient materials, handling, the produce should also be filled to the package rather than the package to the produce. The traditional baskets are often too large and damage occurs during handling and transport and heat of respiration accumulates.

Packing

The desirable pack for most fruits and vegetables is one in which the package is tightly filled without budding or overfilling so that the package not the produce, bears the stacking loads. In India, each piece being put into position by hand to maintain a tight packing and to present the fruit attractively when the package is opened. This time consuming operation requires accurate grading into a range of size classes and has become too costly.

Individual wrapping still has a place as does lining the package, to reduce vibration damage, moisture loss or both. Therefore, the most suitable package would depend on many factors, such as the region, the length and nature of the market chain, methods of handling and transport, environmental conditions, availability and cost of materials. Generally, In India, wooden boxes are used for packing fruit prodce. With the increase in production, the requirement for boxes is also increasing. According to an estimate approximate demand for packing the presently grown fruits alone is around 540 million boxes (20 kg cap.) requiring 50 lakh cum of wood (Chadha and Anand, 1988). It is expected that this demand will double by the end of the century. But, with the depletion of forest resources alternative packaging materials are to be developed which use either less wood or some other under utilizable biomass like cotton sticks, bagasse, paddy straw. At present, corrugated fibre board (CFB) cartons are considered suitable as a substitute for wooden boxes for packing of fruits. More efforts are required for using CFB cartons for packaging of these fruits.

Storage

Storage or stacking of packages must simultaneously ensure stability of stack and provide adequate air movement through the stack to remove respiratory heat. Storage must also be economical of space and easy to achieve. A much stronger package is needed for long distance transport or for high stacking in cool stores than for shot distance and local marketing. Round baskets are more difficult to stack securely without risking damage to the contents.

Consumer Pre-packaging

Pre-packaging means the packaging of the produce in mesh bags or transparent films in small units for retail shops as customers may insist on viewing the produce before purchase. Generally, produce is weighed, packaged and sold as small units. Some times, the packaging of produce in polyethylene films is beneficial as it provides a degree of modified atmosphere due to accumulation of respired CO_2.

Mango

The harvested fruits should be graded according to variety, size, appearance and maturity, although, it is not the usual practice. Ripe and damaged fruits, relatively of poor quality are usually retained for local markets while yellow green fruits are packed for distant places.

Proper packaging is an essential pre-requisite for maintaining good appearance, colour and quality with minimum decay los of the produce or reaching the marketing centre and finally to consumers. In India, baskets made of bamboo, arhar (Cajanus) or mulberry with paddy straw as cushioning material were preferred because of their low cost (Naik, 1949). Basket type of packaging is often found to be unsatisfactory because of uneven ripening of fruits with subdue surface colour development, more shrinkage, bruising and mechanical injury. This leads to higher physiological weight loss and decay loss and unsatisfactory for stacking too during storage and transit. Keeping these in view, it is suggested that conventional cylindrical or conical shape of baskets can eb replaced by rectangular shape of baskets with or without middle tray to utilize maximum storage, transport space and better stackabilities (Chadha and Anand, 1988). These baskets can be reused as they allow nesting of empty baskets to reduce return freight cost (Krishnamurthy, 1988). News paper lining can be used to avoid bruising and better ripening. Regarding paddy straw as cushioning material, Contractor (1951) showed it to be unsatisfactory to avoid bruising injury.

For better quality of fruits ventilated wooden boxes of different sizes have been recommended for packing mangoes. Ventilated lugs, corrugated fibre board boxes of different dimensions, depending upon the variety to be packed have been used in India. The mango cv. Alphonso fruits packed in CFB boxes with partitions exhibited less bruising during transport as compared to those packed in wooden crates with straw and news paper as cushioning materials. The CFB box with partitions showed slow rate of ripening, reduced rate of loss in weight, shriveling and spoilage of the fruits during storage. Further, the fruits packed in CFB boxes with partioner trays also recored less PLW than those packed in CFB boxes with dry grass and news paper or conventional wooden crates with dry grass and news paper.

Wood wool, paddy straw, news paper, dry and soft grasses or excelsior are often used at the bottom and top as cushioning materials. Wrapping of individual fruits in tissue paper and news paper was found suitable for proper ripening and reduced decay loss during storage of mango cvs. Dashehari and Langra. Further, they reported that fruits of mango cv. Langra treated with hot water + 500 ppm MH + 0.1 per cent Bavistin and wrapping of individual fruit in news paper showed minimum decay loss during storage. Moreover, wrapping of individual fruit in tissue paper impregnated with diphenyl is useful in reducing decay loss and damage during transit and storage of fruits. Tissue paper or craft paper linings between layers has also been suggested when fruits are packed in ventilated wooden boxes. Mukherjee and Srivastava (1967) have advocated that wrapping of individual fruits (unipack) in tissue paper was best out of other packaging materials *i.e.*, paper lining, straw along walls, paper between layers, polyethylene bag lines for transport of mango cv. Langra. Although, The pre-packaging of 3 or 4 fruits together in a paper bag exhibited better ripening of fruits and saved labour. They have also of the opinion that polyethylene packing (without ven) is not suitable for mango. However, The pre-packaging of 6 per cent waxed mango in 200 gauge polyethylene with 0.6 per cent ventilation effective in reducing PLW and spoilage at room and low temperature conditions. Pre-packaging and wax emulsion lowered the respiratory activity and extended the shelf life of fruits. Recently, pre-packaging of Neelum mango in 200 gauge polyethylene with or without ethylene absorbant proved advangageous for reduction of decay loss and delayed ripening.

Tested various pal packing media in wooden boxes for short term room storage and studied ripening behaviour of three north India mango varieties. Fruits packed with Dhak leaves (*Butea frondosa*) and sugarcane leaves (*Saccharum officinarum*) showed higher percentage of ripening and better quality in early varieties *i.e.* Gaurjeet and Bombay green. However, in late variety Sukul, Sirus leaves (*Albizzia labbek*), saw dust and wooden box (double layer) produced better effect on ripening and quality of the fruits.

Guava

Being highly perishable in nature, guava fruits should be marketed immediately after harvest as they are liable to deteriorate very fast. Pre-packaging and packings play a vital role in guava handling, storage and transportation. Stored guava successfully upto 6 days in perforated polyethylene bags and wooden boxes without rotting, less weight loss and quality than the fruits kept in basket without any packaging material. Similar response of pre-packaging was also reported. Further studies indicated that waxing in addition to polyethylene packaging have additional effect on prolonging the prolonging the shelf life of guava., Pre-packaging combined with waxing extended the shelf life of guava for 10 days as compared to control, where the shelf life was 5 days only. 150 ppm NAA (Napthalene acetic acid) dip for 5 minutes and packaging in 150 gauge polyethylene with 0.5 per cent vents was best for prolonging the shelf life of Sardar guava fruits. NAA (150 ppm) and Benzyl adenine (15 ppm) were found optimum and effective in arresting ripening process. Optimum radiation dose of 30 krad delayed ripening of guava by 5 days. But when irradiated fruits packed in wax paper and polyethylene film, the delay in ripening was 6 and 7 days, respectively.

A brief report has been given for suitability of packaging material for guavas. The guava leaves with dry soft hay alone and in combination with top covering of basket with qunny sheets. It was found that guava leaves were better than dry soft hay and other combination with gunny sheets in minimizing the total loss.

Banana

The packing of banana in boxes or other containers is not common in India. Generally, the whole bunches are wrapped with banana leaves for internal trade and transport. The wrapping of banana in polyethylene bags helps to reduce bruising due to a lubricant effect of the film and ude to the high humidity around the fingersm preventing damaged areas from drying out and becoming severely necrotic. Banana should be packed in telescopic type CFB boxes of the size 57 × 30 × 22.5 cm and having ten 1.3 cm diameter holes particularly for export purposes.

Citrus

In India, the citrus fruits are harvested by hand at proper maturity to ascertain quality and prolonged shelf life. The harvested fruits are graded on the basis of size and appearance at the site of production. Rapid packing should be done after harvesting followed by grading where high temperature and low relative humidity tend to cause excessive loss of moisture from the harvested fruits. The fruits hould be polished lightly with a piece of cloth before packing.

In India, citrus fruits are usually packed in wooden boxes for transportation to distant markets while for local markets, bamboo baskets of various shapes and gunny bags are common in use. To avoid bruising, paddy straw or soft dry grasses are mostly used as padding. Excessive moisture loss aggravates the problem of destoration on long distance transport which can be reduced by phacing the fruit in polyethylene bags. Better storage of Satgudhi oranges in polyethene packs. Waxed fruit in perforated polyethylene bags can be kept for 85 days in cold storage (0-3°C with RH 85-90 per cent). Kinnow fruits have a poor keeping quality and can not be transported in gunny bags. Recently, the packaging of kinnow fruits (i) in corrugated fibre board carton with and without tray, (ii) wrapped in perforated polyethylene bags and then packed in wooden crates, (iii) in mulberry basket alongwith paper shreds using dry paddy straw as cushioning material and (iv) in bamboo basket alongwith paper shreds using dry paddy straw as cushioning material. All the fruits were pre-treated with 1000 ppm Bavistin. On the basis of total fruit loss, the fruits packed in mulberry baskets showed minimum loss. They further stated that mulberry basket superceeded over the other packages in maintaining appearance and freshness of owing to proper ventilation and adequate mechanical strength. However, fruits were liable to compression injury in such type of baskets.

Different packaging materials and containers were also assessed for transportation and storage of oranges cv. UP Hill oranges. Lining of containers with polyethylene sheets was not effective in preventing the loss in weight of fruits during storage but the value of TSS, acidity and vitamin-C were lesser than other treated fruits. However, packaging of fruits in basket alongwith paddy straw as packing material was highly beneficial in minimizing injury and spoilage of the fruits both during transit and storage as compared to wooden boxes.

Waxed kinnow fruits can be stored upto 40 days at low temperature (2.2 – 4.4°C and RH (85-90 per cent)). If such fruits are packed in polyethylene bags, can successfully be stored at low temperature for 85 days. However, usefulness of polyethylene linings in reduction of transpiration and breakdown of skin tissues in kagzi limes.

The effect of different packagings of enzymatic activity of citrus fruits during storage. The study revealed that the activities of peroxidase and polyphenol oxidase were highest in the fruits packed in gunny bags followed by bamboo baskets and wooden boxes, whereas, the catalase activity showed the reverse trend. It indicated that there may be less availability of oxygen in wooden boxes as compared to other two packagings resulting in slow respiration.

Chapter 3

Varietal Suitability for Processing

Processing of fruits into marketable products requires specified characteristics in a variety which could satisfy processor as well as consumer. The processor's interests are based upon distinct qualities of fruits which are appropriate for different types of products, pickles, pulp, canned slices, chutney, beverages *etc.* The procurement cost is another important factor for the processing industry. Consistent quality of the product at competitive rates are among the parameters considered by the consumer.

1. High Yield

The primary concern would naturally be that the variety must be high yielding so that the procurement cost is most economical. The mango, Totapuri, Beneshan *etc.* are heavy yielders and are available for commercial processing sufficient quantities. There are many excellent varieties of fruits well suited for processing but due to lower yields have remained obscure.

2. Morphological Characteristics

The average weight of the fruit is important in the processing operations. Similar is the case with conformability of fruits. It should be easy to handle to keep the labour cost under limits. The colour characteristics of the fruit should be in line with the final product, for example, mango beverages are preferable with orange yellow to golden yellow colour, minimum fibre content and desirable flavour. For pickles, fibrous varieties may be needed. For dehydration, retention of colour, texture *etc.* during processing and subsequent drying could be considered good. The shape of the fruit should fit into the processing machinery at the same time yielding minimum processing waste.

3. Maturity

Maturity at appropriate time and uniform maturity are desirable characteristics for processing. Most of the fruits should mature simultaneously so that fruits from the entire plant could be harvested at a time and such a condition would be even more compelling where mechanical harvesting is in vogue. Plenty of data is available on the assessment of maturity in several fruits. Parameters like size, external colour, pattern of growth, number of days, heat units, specific gravity and some chemical components have been suggested as maturity indices. However, harvesting of fruits are depending upon the market demand when purely economic factors become the over-riding considerations. In such situations special preservation techniques are to be adopted other wise postharvest losses are very high and the optimum quality may not be achieved. Dashehari mangoes harvested in May could developed insipid taste and shrinkage on ripening.

4. Packaging and Transport

The fruit should have such a shape as to pack easily in appropriate packages. These should be able to withstand transportation to the are of consumption. Lot of fruits are damaged due to bruising during transportation which ultimately result in extensive postharvest losses and total postharvest losses in fruits are estimated to be in the range of 25-40 per cent. Packages for variety of fruits are being developed and standardized. Good degree of progress has been achieved in case of Himachal apples and grapes in Maharashtra while in the remaining fruits the conventional packaging is being used, sometimes, incurring huge losses due to bruising, stacking pressure and subsequent rotting. Corrugated fibre board (CFB) boxes are set to replace wooden boxes. Similarly, in a limited way, plastic carates are in use for specified commodities, particularly with high economic value.

5. Pulp Characteristics

The pulp characteristics are extremely important especially for fruits. The pulp or juice contents represent edible portion of the fruit and its values are higher the better. After extracting pulp, the remaining contents are mostly waste and the processors, at times, have to pay for the disposal of waste as most of the industries do not have definite waste disposal programme.

The consistency of pulp is valuable for the processor as higher consistency means higher pectin strength and it would allow highe dilution for preparation of beverages or alternatively will save energy in case of jams, jellies or paste are the targeted products. With higher pectin strength the setting of jelly *etc.* in faster.

The flavour determines the quality of the final product and so does the good colour. These pulp characters generally transfuse into the final product. The artificial addition of flavour or colour is no match for the original quality. Since there are large number of varieties of fruits with distinct flavours it is difficult to synthesis so many diverse flavours. Moreover, the artificial flavours may not be exactly identical to the original flavours and their preservability may be poor. The artificial colours do not find much favour with the control agencies. Natural colour is a mixture of xanthophylls, carotenes, lycopenes, chlorophylls, anthocynins *etc.* and addition of artificial colours could only be a compromise rather than a useful proposition. Some of the commonly used food colours have now been declared unfit and carcinogenic. The sugar-acid blend is another commercially useful trait for fruits. This character could rather be manipulated with relative ease during processing but natural blends are always preferable.

6. Organoleptic Score

The organoleptic score is the sum total of the taste, appearance, texture, odour *etc.* Several methods of organoleptic score determination have been standardized to evaluate the consumer acceptability of the product. Hedonic scale is commonly used for beverage quality. Any fruit with higher organoleptic score is generally graded good and it may also be suitable for product preparation because such qualities of the fruit are transmitted into the final product. Sensory evaluation of raw material and the final product are greatly useful for determining market acceptabilities.

7. Rheological Properties

Any variety selected for processing should be devoid of any deformity or susceptibility to insects or pests. The variety less suitable for fresh consumption could be most appropriate for processing if it has other characteristics like high yield, good shape and size *etc.* and responds to processing technology.

8. Cost

The economic factor is the foremost while assessing a cultivar for processing. The processor should be able to procure required material at a reasonable cost, quantity and period availability. The cost of handling and processing of the material should be acceptable within limits. Proximity to the production centre is also important.

9. Consumer Acceptability

A product prepared from a variety of fruit if it does not find favoour with the consumer, is not suitable for processing. Varietal screening of fruits for different products is a continuous process and research in the area must be pursued. In India, the processing industry itself is in its infancy, wide ranging programmes of research may be taken up vigorously which is a must for the very survival of the industry.

Actually assessement of varietal suitability for processing may be construed only an initial step. The suitable variety has to be established in the field and in the area agreed upon in cooperation with the processing industry. In this way we can expect consistent quality of the products.

Chapter 4
Storage of Fruits

A complex series of metabolic adjustments occur in fruit crops after harvest which are influenced by dislocation of supply of food nutrients, minerals, water and bio regulators from the parent plant to the harvested produce. Basic respiratory processes are necessary to supply the energy required to maintain the essential repair reactions upon which the integrity and independent existence of the organ depend. Over and above this maintenance metabolism, the harvested produce is able to continue its normal development which may lead to ripening and senescence. In addition, the harvested organ has the ability to respond metabolically to the environment in which it is stored, to wounding and to microbial attack. Such basic biochemical and physiological changes lead to major changes in the chemical composition and physical structure of the tissue and have an important effect on the longevity and quality of the fruit crops. In sub tropical to tropical conditions, 25 to 40 per cent losses result from faulty harvesting and handling improper packing, transportation, storage condition, spoilage and due to microbial attack after harvesting. The dimination of these food losses would have the following advantages.

1. The food supply can be increased without bringing another hectare of land into production and without using greater amounts of energy, water and capital.
2. The wastage of energy used to produce and market the lost food supply will be eliminated.
3. The problem of garbage disposal and consequent pollution will be reduced greatly.
4. Consumer needs will be more fully satisfied and better nutrition will be insured with the same amount of non renewable resources such as land, water, energy and labour.

5. Marketing of the produce will be regulated and resulted in higher remuneration to the producer and longer availability of nutritious and healthy produce to the consumers at reasonable price.

A method to delay ripening and onset of senescence would be of immense value to increase the storeability of produce. Various viable technologies such as improved methods of harvesting, handling, grading, precooling and cold storages, controlled, modified and sub-atmospheric (hypoboric) storages, redurization, use of pre harvest and postharvest application of different chemicals (fungicides, ethylene absorbants, antiethylene agent, antitranspirants, wax emuleions, antioxidants, in package desiccants, senescence retardants, antibiotics, bio-regulaors, calcium *etc.* have been evolved to increase the longevity of produce.

Methods of Storage

1. Method of Harvesting, Handling and Grading

Proper care of harvesting and handling is necessary to preserve subsequent quality of fruits. Faulty harvesting and rough handling at the orchard directly affects the market quality. On storage, bruises and injuries appear first as brown spots which subsequently become black patches making the commodity unattractive. Injuries to the peel or at stalk and serve an avenue for micro-organisms and lead to rotting. Moreover, respiration and engodenous ethylene production increases markedly by the damages, causes early onset of senescence and thus reducing the storage life of the fruit produce. Method of harvesting and handling operations very according to the crop and the region. Generally, different kinds of fruits require different methods of harvesting. Some fruits such as guava, mango and citrus may easily be plucked. Harvesting of fruits using secateurs keeping very small (8-10 mm) pedicel have shown pronounced effect in increasing the shelf life and reduced the decay loss in fruits. Recently, Central Institute for Subtropical Horticulture, Lucknow has developed a mango harvester which is very efficient for harvesting the fruits from height of tree. Proper grading and handling of fruits proved beneficial for transportation, marketing and to fetch high premium. Larger sized mango fruits have better shelf life than smaller ones. Similarly grading on specific gravity basis also indicated that the fruits of mango having specific gravity less than one have longer storability than the fruits having more than 1.0 sp. Gravity. On the other hand, in case of guava, reverse situation exists.

2. Pre-cooling

Pre-cooling refers to the rapid removal of field heat from freshly harvested fruit produce before packing and it also helps in reducing the refrigeration load while storing at low temperature. It reduces weight loss, shrinkage, delay in ripening and retarded ethylene production and restricts enzymatic and respiratory activities. Prompt cooling to required temperature also inhibits growth of decay producing micro-organism. Various methods of pre-cooling *viz.* hydrocooling, vaccum cooling, air cooling, room cooling, forced air cooling and top icing are in practice. In, India no systematic studies have been conducted on the effect of pre-cooling on ripening and storage of fruits. Mango fruits Cv. Dashehari dipped in cooled water (12°C) for 30 minutes and treated with 0.1 per cent Bavistin increased the storability for 7 days at room temperature and 21-25 days at 12°C. Pre-cooling was also found to be effective in reducing the incidence of spongy tissue in Alphanso mango from 20 to 10 per cent. In guava pre-cooling in ice water followed by Waxol-O_{12} coating, extend the shelf life for 2 days. The wastage further reduced when pre cooled fruits stored at 11.1-12.76°C.

3. Zero Energy Cool Chamber Storage

This simple brick sand structure reduced the temperature and increased the relative humidity inside the chamber than out side. Thus, change in environmental factor proved beneficial to minimized the per cent PLW, shriveling and maintained the quality in different crops like ber and citrus. This structure also extend the shelf life of mango in some parts of country like Konkan, Tamilnadu and other places.

4. Packaging

The two main functions of packaging are, to assemble the produce in convenient units for handling and to protect the produce during transportation and marketing operations. The common packages are wooden boxes, wire bound boxes, basket made of bamboo, Arhar (Cajanus) or mulberry of different shapes like conical, cylindrical, telescopic and modified rectangular in shape, corrugated fibre board boxes, plastic containers, jute bags are under practice. Beside this, certain packaging materials like news paper, tissue paper, soft dry hays, paddy straw, wood dust, green leaves and egg trays are commonly used to avoid bruising during transportation, marketing and storage of fruit produce.

In most parts of India, baskets with paddy straw as cushioning material were preferred because of their low cost. But such packages are found to be unsatisfactory because of uneven ripening of fruits with sub due surface colour development. For better quality of fruits, ventilated wooden boxes of different sizes have been recommended for packing mangoes. In recent years, CFB boxes have been found best because it slowed down the rate of ripening, reduced rate of loss in weight, shriveling and spoilage of fruits during storage. Now, unipack system is getting importance as it reduced the spoilage during storage and transport. Even some scientist have advocated that pre packaging of 3 or 4 fruits together in a paper bag exhibited better ripening of fruits and saved labour. However, polyethylene packing is not suitable for mango. For citrus, fruits are usually packed in wooden boxes for transportation to distant markets while for local markets, bamboo baskets of various shapes and gunny bags are common in use.

5. Low Temperature Storage

Reduction in storage temperature is one of the most important methods of prolonging the shelf life of fruits. Physiological responses of fruits to declining temperature vary considerably. Basically, it reduces the respiration and general metabolism and thus resulted in longer storage life. The maintenance of high relative humidity is also important to maintain the freshness of the product and conserve the fruit quality. Storage of fruits at high relative humidity may, however, predispose the produce to infection by microbial pathogens causing postharvest decays and rots.

The oprimum low temperature of 12-15°C is most effective temperature to extend the storability of mango fruits for 25-30 days depending on the cultivars. However, green ripe guavas can be stored in marketable condition at 8° to 10°C and 85 to 90 per cent relative humidity for 2 to 5 weeks. Storage of citrus fruits at low temperature is the most effective useful method for delaying the development of decay. It retard the development of decay both by maintaining the resistance of the host and also by retarding the growth of the pathogen. Similarly, other fruit produce also exhibited positive response with low temperature in relation to longevity.

6. Controlled Atmosphere Storage

Addition or removal of cases resulting in an alteration in atmospheric composition different in that of normal air such as in CA, MA or hypoboric (low pressure) storage which has been employed to extend the storage life of fruits, as an adjunt to low temperature storage. This methods reduced the respiration and other metabolic reactions mainly due to increase in CO_2 and decrease in O_2 concentrations. CA storage with high CO_2 inhibits breakdown of pectic substances and retain fruit texture and firmness for a longer period and retention of flavour may also be improved. Alphanso mangoes kept in an atmosphere of 7.5 per cent CO_2 at 8.3 to 10°C for 35 days and Raspuri mangoes stored under similar conditions at 5.5 to 7.2°C for 49 days were unimpaired and ripened satisfactorily within 3 days after removal from storage. Higher CO_2 concentrations caused injury in terms of fermentative decarboxylation with the formation of aldehyde and R_O H end products which impaired the consumer's acceptability.

7. Sub Atmospheric Pressure Storage

Ripening of the mango fruits can be delayed to extends its storage life by reducing the pressure in the storage chamber before 100 mm Hg, control fruit stored at 760 mm Hg started to ripen after16 days in storage at 13°C, whereas, fruits stored at 100 and 75 mm Hg started to ripen after 25 and 35 days. All fruits stored to ripen after 25 and 35 days. All fruits stored at sub atmospheric pressure ripened in 3 to 4 days after transfer in normal storage at 25°C.

8. Heat Treatment

Immersing of mango fruits in hot water (52° to 54°C) treatment for 10 to 30 minute control the postharvest diseases particularly Anthracnose in mango. The combined treatment of 1000 ppm with hot water treatment controlled the decay loss and conteracted with the accelerated ripening caused by hot water.

9. Chemical Modifications

The chemicals include all categories of plant hormones, growth retardants inhibitors, C_2E_4 absorbants, waxes which delayed ripening and senescence. Beside these chemicals fungicides, antibiotics and minerals like calcium are also found potent to reduce the postharvest losses and increased the longevity of harvested produce. Plant hormones like IBA, GA and BA delayed the ripening and onset of senescence. Similarly, growth retardants like MH, CCC, Alar and morphactin also delayed the ripening, pre and postharvest application of calcium compounds like calcium nitrate and calcium chloride found effective to extend the shelf life of mango, guava and other horticultural crops. The calcium application reduced the weight loss, CO_2, C_2H_4 production, maintained the firmness and minimized the decay loss. Use of Potassium permanganate as ethylene absorbant in banana and guava also found to be effective to minimized the postharvest losses and maintain the firmness and quality of fruits for longer period.

10. Irradiation

The preservation and extension of the fresh produce by irradiation is of considerable interest. Irradiation is found useful to disinfect the produce of fruit files and other insect-pests and to extend the shelflife of produce by restricting the growth of pathogenic organisms and slowing down the rate of metabolism of the produce. In addition to this, irradiation has been found to be of great practical significance in controlling sprouting. Such irradiated produce maintain its quality for prolonged period.

Chapter 5

Postharvest Handling

After harvesting, fruits are liable to accelerated physiological, chemical and microbial processes that invariably lead to deterioration and loss of wholesomeness. So, postharvest physiology mainly deals with the basic physiological changes and underlying mechanisms that occur in a detached plant part or organ during handling, storage and marketing. Scientifically, postharvest physiology is a division of plant biology which deals with physiological and biochemical processes in plant material after harvest and that are handled and marketed in the living state. In postharvest physiology one consider mature and ripe to be distinct terms for different stages of fruit development. Mature is best defined by as "having completed natural growth and development". Most postharvest technologists consider that the definition should be "that stage at which a commodity has reached a sufficient stage of development that after harvesting and postharvest handling (including ripening, where required), its quality will be at least the minimum acceptable to the ultimate consumer".

Postharvest Handling of Fruit Produce

Fruit is live tissues harvested at various stages of growth and development, have tender texture, contain high moisture (60-95 per cent) and water activity, loose water to the surrounding atmosphere and continue respiration which produces heat and water at the expense of food reserves, carbohydrates, proteins, lipids *etc.* So, the postharvest period begins with the separation of plant organs as food items from the medium of its immediate growth or production and ends when the food enters the process of preparation for final consumption or further preservation. When plant materials are attached to the parent plant (before harvest), losses due to respiration and transpiration are replaced by photosynthates, water and minerals supplied from the plant. However, after harvest, the product is dependent entirely on its own food reserves and water content. Losses of water and substrates used in respiration can no longer be replaced and deterioration of the product begins. Generally, fruits pass through five distinct phases:

(a) Development *i.e.*, morphological and chemical completion of tissue.

(b) Young or premature *i.e.*, development period before the onset of maturation.

(c) Mature *i.e.*, completion or fullness of growth and edible quality, most of the maturation processes must be completed while the produce is still attached to the plant.

(d) Ripe *i.e.*, maximum aesthetic and edible quality.

(e) Senescence *i.e.*, produce is worthless and inedible.

The large amount of starch, acid and phenolics present in the flesh of young or premature fruits make them inedible. At the young stage, flesh contains little sugar *i.e.*, glucose fructose or sucrose. The flesh cells enlarge considerably and sugar content increases while starch, acid and phenolic content decreases as the fruit approach maturity. In addition, certain volatile compounds develop, giving the fruit its characteristics aroma and flavour. Chlorophyll degradation (loss of green colour) and synthesis of carotenoids (yellow and orange colour) and anthocyanins (red and blue colour) take place both in the skin and flesh with fruit ripening. All fruits soften as they ripen due to changes in cell wall composition and structure.

Table 2: Compositional Changes in the Fruit Produce after Harvesting

Changes	*Processes*	*Examples and Significance*
Weight loss	Water loss, transpiration, respiration and evaporation.	Unattractive appearance, texture changes, shrivelling
Carbohydrate conversion	Starch converts to sugar, sugar converts to starch (lemon), Enzymatic.	Change beneficial in Pear and persimmons and Banana.
Softening/ Hardening- change in texture	Softening due to enzymatic reaction of pectin methyl esterase, Toughening due to fibre development.	Beneficial in Pear, banana and apple but after sometime detrimental.
Change in colour	Due to both pigment synthesis and destruction. Colour-anthocyanin, carotenoids and their derivatives.	Beneficial in apple, pear, banana, citrus but detrimental in litchi due to browning.
Change in vitamins	Enzymatic processes, gain in vitamin A, loss in vitamin C after harvesting.	—

History of Postharvest Physiology of Fruits

1. Kids and West (1930). From Cambridge University, England first time coined the term climacteric.
2. Biale and Young (1950). From University of California, Los Angles, USA describe about ethylene analysis.
3. Burg (1955). From Harvard University, USA describe about ethylene analysis based on gas chromatography.
4. Lieberman (1960). From USDA, USA, ethylene biosynthesis from methionine.

5. Smock (1965). From Cornell University, USA gave an idea about controlled atmospheric storage.
6. Biale (1960). Gave two terms climacteric and non-climacteric based on respiratory behaviour of fruits.
7. Lutz and Hardenberg (1968). From Germany classify the fruits on the basis of period of growing season.
8. Yang (1970). From University of California, Divas, USA worked on ethylene biosynthesis from methionine to ethylene ACC (1-amino cyclopropane 1-carboxylic acid) (immediate processor).
9. Biale and Young (1981). Gave the most accepted differentiation between climacteric and non-climacteric fruits on the basis of respiratory pattern and ethylene synthesis.
10. Kader (1980). From University of California, USA worked on CA storage and quality concept in fruits.
11. Watada *et al.* (1984). Gave the stages of development and senescence based on physiological processes and usage of fruit crops.

Terminology for the Description of Developmental Stages of Fruit Crops

(1) Gortner *et al.* (1967)

(a) **Development** – Increase in physical attributes (size, weight, volume) and morphology.

(b) **Pre-maturation** – Even though size, shape are good, qualitative changes have started but it is not accepted by majority. The stage of maturation that begins before the fruit has completed its developmental process is called pre-maturation.

(c) **Maturation** – Most of the growth is completed.

(d) **Ripening** – Terminal stage of maturity.

(e) **Senescence** – Last stage of ripening, loss of characteristics flavour and palatability.

2. Ryall and Lipton (1972): Repetition of Gortner's terms.

The clearly said that although development includes predominant increment in size, weight and volume, a major initial portion of development consisted of pre-maturation while maturity included a part of the developmental processes and a part during the post development processes. Ripening which was the terminal stage of maturity consisted of that stage when no development was taking place in the fruit. This was a period of maximum usefulness to the consumers. Senescence is as short as a stage of ripening and is the beginning of the degradative changes. Deterioration can set at any stage of growth when it becomes unfit and that may be because of any external agents.

3. Watada *et al.* (1984)

He revealed that development includes all stages from initiation to death. The gave the folloging classes or stages of growth (Figure 2).

(i) **Development:** The series of processes from the initiation of growth to death of a plant or plant part.

(ii) **Growth:** The irreversible increase in physical attributes of a developing plant or plant part.

(iii) **Maturation:** The maturation is a wide term and it is that stage of development which leads to the attainment of physiological or horticultural maturity.

(*a*) **Physiological maturity:** The stage of development when a plant or plant part will continue ontogeny even if detached.

(*b*) **Horticultural maturity:** The stage of development when a plant or plant part possesses the prerequisite for utilization by consumers for a particular purpose.

The term horticulture maturity is defined on a relative scheme as suggested by Ryall and Lipton (1979) because the term can refer to any stage of development *e.g.*, sprouts or seedlings are horticulturally mature in the early stage of development whereas most vegetative, inflorescence, flowers, fruits and underground storage organs become horticulturally mature in the mid stage and seeds and nuts in the late stage of development.

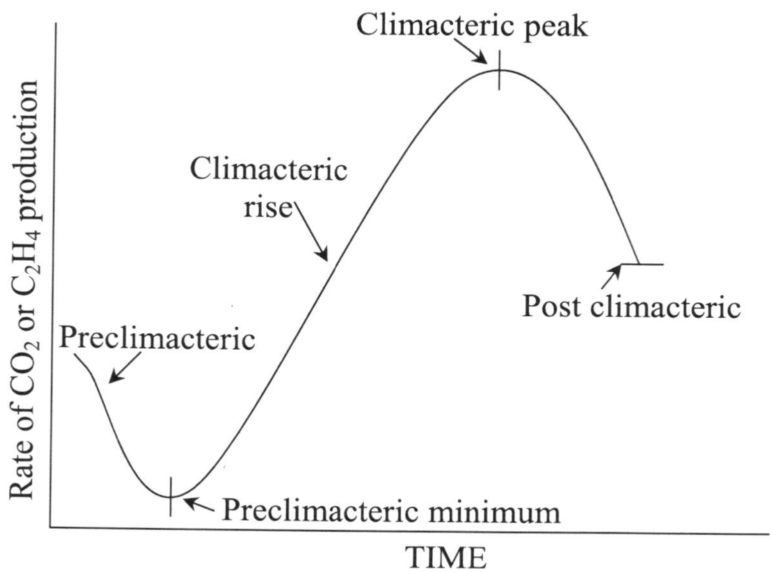

Figure 1: Phases of Climacteric Period.

(iv) Ripening: It is the shortest stage in terms of duration when the fruit has optimal quality for consumption. In general ripening may be considered as the changes taking place from the final stage of fruit development through the early stage of its senescence and relates mainly to fleshy fruits and results in characteristics aesthetic and/or food quality. In other words, ripening is the composite of the processes that occur from the later stages of growth and development through the early stages of senescence and those results in characteristics aesthetic and/or food quality, as evidenced by changes in composition, colour, texture or other sensory attributes.

(v) Climacteric period: The period in the development of some plant parts that involves a series of biochemical changes associated with the natural respiratory rise and autocatalytic production of ethylene. The climacteric period consist of the preclimacteric, preclimacteric minimum, climacteric rise, climacteric peak and post climacteric phases.

(vi) Ageing: Any increment of time which may (or may not) be accompanied by physiological change. The connotation of ageing in a scientific context can differ from that of common usage where aging is equated with senescence. In science, the term aging is used when material such as tissue slices,

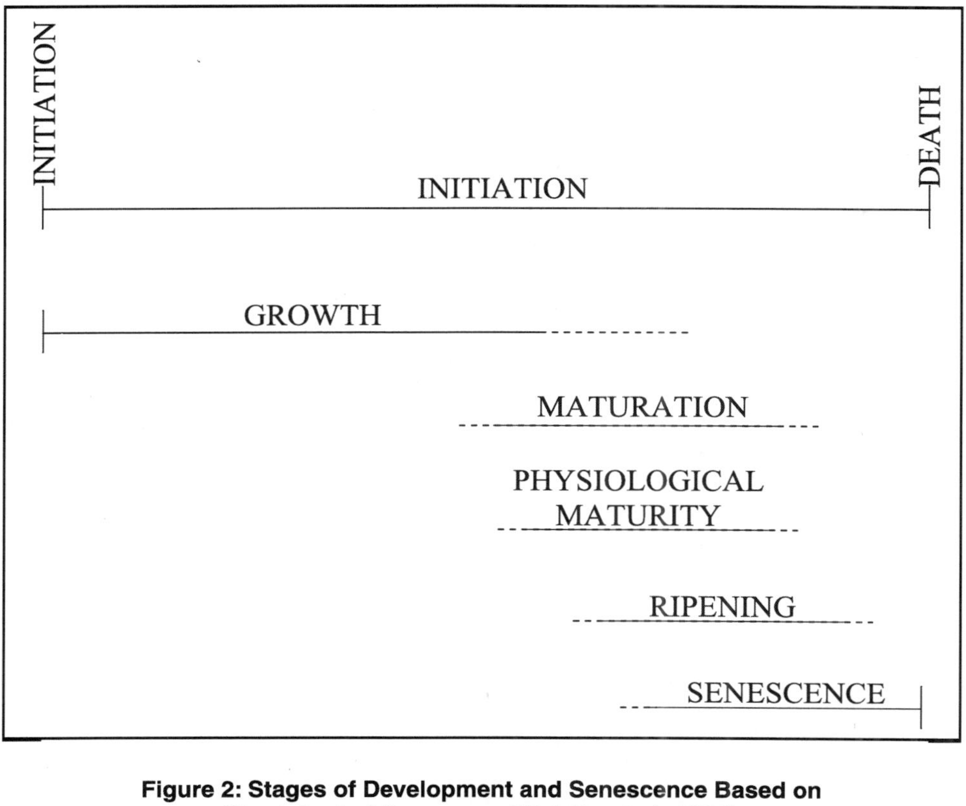

Figure 2: Stages of Development and Senescence Based on Physiological Processes (Watada *et al.,* 1984).

extracts, organelles and even some mature but unharvested fruit (*e.g.*, avocado) may age in that necessarily undergoing changes as associated with physiological senescence.

(vii) Senescence: Those processes that follow physiological maturity or horticultural maturity and lead to death of tissue.

The stages of development can overlap, as indicated by broken lines at the ends of the solid lines in Figure 2. For example, growth of most fruit ceases by the early stages of maturation but growth of some fruits, such as apples and pear, continues through maturation and into the initial part of ripening. "Physiological maturity" and "ripening" are phenomenon generally observed with many fruits and some flowers but generally not with other organs such as roots, foliage, stems and tubers.

Chapter 6

Postharvest Classification of Fruits

Attempts have been made from time to time since 1960 to classify the fruits according to their postharvest physiology and storage behaviour.

A.

The first system of classification was given by Biale (1960) where he classified the fruits into two categories according to their respiratory behaviour during ripening:

(i) **Climacteric fruits***e.g.*, Apple, Apricot, Avocado, Banana, Cherimoya, Fig, Guava, Jackfruit, Kiwifruit, Mango, Muskmelon.

(ii) **Non-climacteric fruits***e.g.*, Cherry, Grape, Grapefruit, Lemon, Lime, Orange, Pineapple, Strawberry, Litchi, Ber.

B.

Lutz and Hardenburg (1968) tried to correlate the storage life of fruits with their growing season. Those that is most perishable *e.g.*, Strawberries have a very short growing season and those that have a long storage life (winesap apple) have a long growing season (Table 3).

Table 3

Sl.No.	*Fruits*	*Number of Days (Full bloom to harvest)*	*Normal Storage Life (Days)*
1.	Strawberries	24-28	5-7
2.	**Cherries:** Black	57	14
	Bing	71	14
	Napolean	68	14

Sl.No.	*Fruits*	*Number of Days (Full bloom to harvest)*	*Normal Storage Life (Days)*
3.	**Apple:** Winesap	160-170	150-180
	Jonathan	140-145	90-60
	Yellow transparent	70-75	60-70
4.	**Pears:** Bartlett	110-130	75-90
	Bose	130-145	90-105
	Anjou	145-150	120-180
5.	Peach	122	14
		128	21-29
6.	Apricot (Royal)	100	7-21

It is evident from the table that there is some consistent correlation in growth period and storage time *e.g.*, Strawberry growing period is short so storage period is also in least days. In cherry, growing period is 57 days and storage period is 14 days and in apple growing is long so storage period is also long.

This system did not work as in Peach and apricot including certain cultivar of cherry the relationship of days of maturity and storage life did not hold well.

They classified the fruits into three categories on the basis of relation between ripening and drift of CO_2 production of fruits.

(i) **Gradual decrease type:** Fruits in which the respiratory rate gradually decreases throughout the ripening process *e.g.*, Citrus fruits.

(ii) **The temporary rise type:** In this type, the respiratory rate increases temporarily and full ripeness occurs after peak of respiration. *E.g.*, Banana, Avocado *etc.*

(iii) **The late peak type:** In this type the medium rate of respiration is shown from full ripe to over ripe stage *e.g.*, Japanese persimmon, strawberry, peach *etc.*

This proved to be most useful classification.

C.

Wolfgang Holl (1977): He tried to establish the relationship between the respiratory patterns of fruit with their predominant pigment. He reported that:

(a) The fruits with carotenoids pigments were associated with the climacteric fruits *e.g.*, Mango.

(b) The fruits with anthocyanins pigments were associated with the non-climacteric fruits.

But his theory was rejected as soon as it was released.

D.

Watada *et al.* (1984): They classified the fruits into 2 groups:

(a) Those harvested when partially developed and physiological immature *e.g.*, Grape, Mango, apple, avocado *etc.*

(b) Those harvested when fully developed and physiologically mature or even ripe *e.g.*, Grape, litchi, cherries *etc.* This system also could not accepted.

E.

Biale and Young (1981): They have given the most accepted postharvest classification of fruits depending on their respiratory behaviour during ripening. They classified fruits into two categories *i.e.*, climacteric and non-climacteric and differentiated as following Table 4.

Table 4

Climacteric	*Non-climacteric*
At the end of growth undergo a large increase in respiration accompanied by marked changes in composition and texture of fruits. Ripening is associated with a large increase in ethylene production. The increase in respiration and ethylene production can be induced prematurely in climacteric fruits by treating them with a suitable concentration of ethylene or other unsaturated hydrocarbon like propylene. Ripening process is irreversible once the endogenous (autocatalytic) C_2H_4 production increased to certain level.	Show no change in respiration that can be associated with distinct changes in composition. An unnatural climacteric like respiratory increase can be induced by treating with C_2H_4 or other unsaturated hydrocarbon yet this increased respiration is not accompanied by an increase in endogenous ethylene production and other respiration rate usually subsides whereas increase rapidly upon the removal of exogenous ethylene or other unsaturated hydrocarbon. However, ethylene treatment does not accelerate senescence in non-climacteric fruits.

Again they classified the climacteric fruits into 2 types:

(a) Type I fruit: Ethylene concentration clearly rises before the onset of ripening as shown by the respiratory increase *e.g.*, Banana.

(b) Type II fruit: In which rise in ethylene production does not occur prior to the onset of ripening *e.g.*, Apple, avocado, cherry *etc.*

F.

Classification of Horticultural commodities according to their respiration rates.

Table 5

Class	*Commodity*
Very low	Dried fruits, nuts.
Low	Apple, grapes.
Moderate	Apricot, figs, peach, pear, nectarine, plum.

G.

Kader and Maris (1977) classify the fresh fruit produce according to their relative perishability and potential storage life.

Table 6: Classification of Fresh Fruit Crops According to their Relative Perishability and Potential Storage Life in Air at Near Optimum Temperature and Relative Humidity

Relative Perishability	*Potential Storage Life (Weeks)*	*Commodities*
Very high	<2	Apricot, blackberry, blueberry, cherry, fig, raspberry, strawberry, sweet corn processed fruits.
High	2-4	Avocado, banana, grape (without SO_2 treatment), guava, loquat, mandarin, mango, nectarine, papaya, peach, plum.
Moderate	4-8	Apple and pear (some cultivars), grape (SO_2-treated), orange, grapefruit, lime, kiwifruit, persimmon, pomegranate.
Low	8-16	Apple and pear (some cultivars), lemon.
Very low	>16	Tree nuts, dried fruits.

H.

Wills *et al.* (1998) classify some edible fruits according to presence or absence of a respiration climacteric during ripening.

Table 7: Classification of some Edible Fruits According to Presence or Absence of a Respiration Climacteric during Ripening

Climacteric Fruits	*Non-climacteric Fruits*
Apple (*Malus domestica*)	Bell pepper (*Capsicum* spp.)
Apricot (*Prunus armeniaca*)	Carambola (*Averrhoa carambola*)
Asian pear (*Pyrus pyrifolia*)[a]	Cherry (*Prunus* spp.)
Avocado (*Persea americana*)	*Citrus* spp.[a]
Banana (*Musa* spp.)	Grape (*Vitis vinifera*)
Blackberry (*Rubus occidentalis*)	Litchi (*Litchi chinensis*)
Blueberry and Cranberry (*Vaccinium* spp.)[a]	Pineapple (*Ananas comosus*)
Cherimoya (*Annona cherimola*)	—
—	Rambutan (*Nephelium lappaceum*) Strawberry (*Fragaria* spp)
Feijoa (*Feijoa sellowiana*)	—
Fig (*Ficus carica*)	—
Guava (*Psidium guajava*)	—
Jujube (*Ziziphus jujube*)	—
Kiwifruit (*Actinidia deliciosa*)	—
Mango (*Mangifera indica*)	—

Climacteric Fruits	*Non-climacteric Fruits*
Papaya (*Carica papaya*)	—
Passionfruit (*Passiflora edulis*)	—
Peach (*Prunus persica*)	—
Pear (*Pyrus communis*)	
Persimmon (*Diospyros kaki*)	Oliva (*Olea eurapaea*).
Plum (*Prunus domestica, Prunus salicina*)	—
Raspberry (*Rubus ideus*)	—
Sapota (*Calocarpum sapota*)	—

Chapter 7

Process of Maturity and Maturity Standards

Maturity at harvest is the most important factor that determines storage life and final fruit quality. Immature fruits are more subject to shriveling and mechanical damage and are of inferior quality when ripened. Over-ripe fruits are likely to become soft and develop insipid flavour soon after harvest. Fruit picked either too early or too late in the season are more susceptible to physiological disorders and have a shorten storage life than those picked at mid-season. Maturity also influences susceptibility of the fruit to water loss and mechanical injury. Fruits harvested too early may lack flavour and may not ripen properly while produce harvested too late may be fibrous or have very limited market life. Therefore, harvesting of fruits at proper stage of maturity is of paramount importance for attaining desirable quality. The level of maturity actually helps in selection of storage methods, estimation of shelf life, selection of processing operations for value addition *etc*. The maturity has been divided into two categories:

(i) Physiological Maturity

When a plant or plant parts will continue ontogeny even if detached.

(ii) Horticultural Maturity

It refers to the stage of development when palnt and plant part possesses the pre-requisites for use by consumers for a particular purpose *i.e.*, ready for harvest or in other words, it is a developmental state of a fruit on the tree or plant which will result in a satisfactory product after harvest. It may be categorized as:

(a) **Dessert Maturity:** for local market, best optimum quality for the specific purpose. This term is used mainly with reference to fruits.

(b) **Shipping maturity:** for export purpose.

(c) **Processing maturity:** for value addition.

(d) **Culinary maturity**: for used as raw.

Related Terminology

(i) **Mature:** It is derived from Latin word "*Maturus*" which means ripen. It is that stage of fruit development, which ensures attainment of maximum edible quality at the completion of ripening process.

(ii) **Maturation:** It is the developmental process by which the fruit attains maturity. It is the transient phase of development from near completion of physical growth to attainment of physiological maturity. There are different stages of maturation *e.g.*, Immature, mature, optimally mature, over mature.

(iii) **Ripe:** This is the condition of maximum edible quality attained by the fruit following harvest. Only fruit which becomes mature before harvest can become ripe.

(iv) **Ripening:** Ripening involves a series of changes occurring during early stages of senescence of fruits in which structure and composition of unripe fruit is so altered that it becomes acceptable to eat. Ripening is a complex physiological process resulting in softening, colouring, sweetening and increases in aroma compounds so that ripening fruits are ready to eat or process. The associated physiological or biochemical changes are increased rate of respiration and ethylene production, loss of chlorophyll and continued expansion of cells and conversion of complex metabolites into simple molecules.

(v) **Senescence:** Senescence can be defined as the final phase in the ontogeny of the plant organ during which a series of essentially irreversible events occur which ultimately leads to cellular breakdown and death.

Changes in Fruit during Maturity

(i) Increase in sugar.

(ii) Decrease in acidity.

(iii) Decrease in starch *e.g.*, Apple, pear, banana.

(iv) Increase in oil content *e.g.*, Avocado, nuts *etc.*

(v) Changes in pectin constituent resulting into softening.

(vi) Loss of tannins and astringency *e.g.*, persimmon.

(vii) Development of volatiles causing flavour and aroma.

(viii) Loss of chlorophyll in skin and flesh and formation of new pigments.

(ix) Increase in ascorbic acid followed by decrease.

(x) Increase in TSS and sugar content.

(xi) Marked loss of moisture in nuts.

Factors affecting Maturity

I. Internal Factors

(a) Variety.

(b) Stage of development at harvesting.

II. External Factors

(a) Climate and season effects *e.g.*, Temperature, light, humidity, incidence of pests and diseases.

(b) Position of the trees.

(c) Cultural factors *e.g.*, Soil type, soil moisture, water, soil aeration, soil texture and structure, pH, training and pruning methods, rootstocks, plant growth regulators, chemicals, intercropping.

Maturity Index

Any physical or chemical parameter of the fruit which changes with the time during its development in quantity and quality which are highly correlated with the date of maturation and fruit quality is termed as maturity index. Commonly selected horticultural maturity indices include firmness, skin colour, flesh colour, accumulation during specific periods during the growing season are also used. In other cases such as in bananas a physicalchange is used and the fruit is harvested when ridges on the surface of the skin change from angular to round. In practice, any analytical or physical measurement that changes with physiological development and relates to customer acceptance has potential as a maturity index. The maturity index should be easily determined, use simple equipment and provide good correlation with efficacy in final use.

Methods of Maturity Indices and their Component

There may be six methods of maturity indices:

(i) Visual Means

It is like size and shape, colour of the skin, visual appearance, presence of dried outer mature leaves, drying of the plant body, fullness of the fruit *etc.*

(a) Size and Shape

Maturity of fruits can be assessed by their final shape and size at the time of harvest. Fruit shape may be used in some instances to decide maturity. For example, the fullness of cheeks adjacent to pedicel may be used as a guide to maturity of mango and some stone fruits. Some cultivars of banana become less angular in cross section as development and maturation progress. Size is generally of limited value as a maturity index in fruits. With these produce, size is often specified as a quality standard, with large size generally indicating commercial over-maturity and under-sized produce indicating an immature state. The assumption, however, is not always a reliable guide for all-purpose.

(b) Appearance

The visual appearance of fruit is the most important quality factor, which decides its price in the market. The consumer (wholesaler or retailer) observes the quality of fresh fruits with their visual or external appearance. The produce should stain proper shape and size. Medium size produce is always preferred by the consumers, because they tend to view large fruits as more mature. The appearance of the product is the most critical factor in the initial purchase while subsequent purchase may be more related to texture and flavour.

Table 8: Selected Maturity Indicators for Several Fruit Commodities

Commodities	*Maturity indicators*
Almonds	Splitting of hull, separation of hull from shell, development of abscission zone.
Apple	Skin and flesh coloiur, flesh firmness, sugars (soluble solids), acid, starch, days from full bloom to harvest.
Apricot	Dependent on intended purpose (fresh market, canning *etc.*), soluble solids flesh firmness, light transmission properties. Barium yellow skin colour, TSS 10 per cent at ripening.
Asian Pear	Skin colour change from green to yellowish green.
Avocado	Oil content.
Banana	Disappearance of angularity of the finger, drying of top leaves.
Baggugosha	145 days after fruit set.
Ber	Colour break stage (when light yellow colour appear).
Blueberries	Freedom from injury and decay, plump, firm, uniformly blue colour. Green or red indicator of immaturity (unripeness), soft texture may be indicator of over maturity.
Cashewnut	Two months after pollination.
Cherries	Colour change light red to black, soluble solids to 18 per cent -22 per cent, flesh firmness, light transmission properties. TSS 14-15 per cent, light red colour, specific gravity.
Citrus	Fruit colour, taste (both termed unreliable), soluble solids. Soluble solids: acid ratio.
Grapes	Sugar accumulation, loss of acids, berry softening, skin coloration, ripening with varietal flavour/colour development. Translucent bloom on surface, Minimum TSS of 14 to 17.55 per cent, depending on cultivars.
Guava	Colour break stage (when skin colour changes from dark green to light green).
Jackfruit	Spines become well developed and wide spaced.
Kinnow	TSS : acid ratio 12:1 to 14:1.
Kiwi fruit	TSS-6.5 per cent, firmness = 6.1 kg.
Lemon	Thirty or more juice by volume.
Litchi	TSS: acid ratio of 30-40, flattening of tubercles, bright red in colour.
Mango	Changes in shape (increase fullness of cheeks or bulge of shoulder), flesh colour yellow to yellowish-orange.
Papaya	Skin shows yellowing, latex become almost watery at maturity.
Pear	Flesh firmness, ease of spur separation, days from full bloom (indices vary with variety). Harvested hard-green, ripened off the tree; colour, texture, sweetness, typical varietal flavour development.

Commodities	*Maturity indicators*
Peach	Days after full bloom, size, firmness, ground colour, sugars acidity, starch.
Pineapple	Flattening of eyes.
Plums	Skin colour changes, 'Kala Amritsari': 84 days after fruit set, 'Santa Rosa': 94-103 days after full bloom.
Pomegranate	Skin colour yellowish or pink to red, minimum 1.85 per cent titratable acidity.
Strawberry	Fully red at least ¾ of berry surface red or pink.
'Golden Delicious'	12 per cent TSS, 8.3 kg. firmness.
'Red Delicious'	11 per cent TSS, 8.3 kg. firmness.
Pathar Nakh	135 days after fruit set.
Walnut	When hulls plit.

Reid (1995) provides some examples of maturity indices in the following way:

Index	*Examples*
Elapsed days from full bloom to harvest	Apples, pears.
Mean heat units during development	Apple.
Development of abscission layer	Apple.
Surface morphology and structure	Cuticle formation on grapes. Gloss of some fruits (development of wax).
Size	All fruits
Specific gravity	Cherries.
Shape	Angularity of banana fingers, full cheeks of mangoes.
Textural properties	
Firmness	Apples, pears, stone fruits.
Colour, external	All fruits.
Internal colour and structure	Flesh colour of some fruits
Compositional factors	
Starch content	Apples, pears.
Sugar content	Apples, pears, stone fruits, grapes.
Acid content, sugar: acid ratio	Pomegranates, citrus, papaya, kiwifruit.
Juice content	Citrus fruits.
Oil content	Avocados.
Astringency (tannin content)	Persimmons, dates.
Internal ethylene concentration	Apples, pears.

(c) Colour

The loss of green colour of many fruits is a valuable guide to maturity. There is initially a gradual loss in intensity of colour from deep green to lighter green and with many commodities, a complete loss of green colour with the development of yellow, red or purple pigments. Ground colour as measured by colour charts, is useful index of maturity for apple, pear and stone fruits, but is not entirely reliable as it is influenced by factors other than maturity. For some fruits, as they mature on the tree, development of blush colour that is additional colour superimposed on the ground colour can be a good indiator of maturity. Examples are red or red-streaked apple cultivars and red blush on some cultivars of peach.

Some other examples of visual indices are:

(a) Drying of top leaves in banana.
(b) Yellowing of last leaf of peduncle in jackfruit.
(c) Flow of sap from the cut fruit stock slow down if harvesting done after maturity in mango.
(d) Latex become watery on maturity in papaya.
(e) The flow gets decreased on maturity in sapota.
(f) Translucent bloom develop on surface in grape.
(g) Development of angularity in banana.
(h) Flattening of eyes of pineapple.
(i) Flattering of tubercles in litchi.
(j) Spines become well developed and widely spaced at maturity in jackfruit.
(k) Deep purple/black colour develops on skin in jamun.

(ii) Physical Means

(a) Ease of Separation or Abscission

Natural separation of fruits from tree *i.e.*, 'Tapka' in mango should be harvested at the formation of abscission layer.

(b) Firmness

As fruit mature and ripen they soften by dissolution of the middle lamella of the cell walls. The degree of firmness can be estimated subjectively by finger or thumb pressure but more precise objective measurement is possible with pressure tester or penetrometer. In many fruits such as apple, pear, peach, plum, guava and kinnow *etc.* firmness can be used to determine harvest maturity. Penetrometer measures the pressure necessary to force a plunger of specified size into the pulp of the fruit. Such pressure is measured in kilograms force.

(c) Specific Gravity

As fruit mature, their specific gravity increases. This parameter is rarely used in practice to determine when to harvest a crop but it could be where it is possible to develop a suitable sampling technique. It is used, however, to grade crops into different maturities. To do this the fruit is placed in a pot of water; those that flot will be less mature than those that sink.

(iii) Chemical Means

(a) Total Soluble Solids (TSS)

The total soluble solids of the fruit can be measured with refractometer which indicate the harvest maturity of fruits.

(b) Acidity

Acidity is readily determined on a sample of extracted juice by titration with 0.1 N NaOH to the pink end point using phenolphthalein as an indicator. The results are commonly expressed in terms of the dominant organic acid expected in the sample like malic acid for apples or tartaric acid for grapes.

(c) TSS/Acid Ratio

The TSS/acid ratio is a key characteristic determining the taste, texture and feel of fruit segments. It is the sugar/acid ratio which contributes towards giving many fruits their characteristic flavour. It is also an indicator of commercial and sensory ripeness. At the beginning of the ripening process, the sugar/acid ratio is low because of low sugar content and high fruit acid content, this makes the fruit taste sour. During the ripening process, the fruit acids are degraded, the sugar content increases and the sugar/acid ratio achieves a higher value.

(d) Sugars

In climacteric fruits, carbohydrates accumulate during maturation in the form of starch. As the fruit ripens, starch is broken down into sugar. In non-climacteric fruits, sugar tends to accumulate during maturation. A quick method to measure the amount of sugar present in fruits is with a brix hydrometer or a refractometer. This is equivalent to the total amount of soluble solids or sugar content. This factor is used in many parts of the world to specify maturity. This a laboratory technique, however, and might not be suitable for village level production.

(e) Sugar : Acid Ratio

The sugar : acid or TSS : acid ratio is often better related to palatability of fruit than either sugar or acid level alone. Acid levels decrease and the result is an increased perception of sweetness as the sugar : acid ratio increases.

(f) Starch Content

The conversion of starch to sugars during maturation is a simple test for the maturity of some apple cultivars. It is based on the reaction between starch and iodine to produce a blue or purple colour. The method involves cutting the fruit in two helps and dipping the cut pieces into a solution containing 4 per cent potassium iodide and 1 per cent iodine. The cut surfaces stain to a blue-black colour in places where starch is present. Starch converts into sugar as harvest time approaches. Harvest begins when the samples show that 65-70 per cent of the cut surfaces have turned blue-black.

(g) Tannin Content

It determine astringency in some fruits like persimmon.

(h) Oil Content

Oil content can be used to determine the maturity of fruits, such as avocados at the time of harvest and at any time thereafter. Thus, the oil content of an avocado is related to moisture content. The oil content is determined by weighing 5-10 g of avocado pulp and then extracting the oil with a solvent (*e.g.*, benzene or petroleium ether) in a distillation column. This method has been successful for cultivars naurally high in oil content.

(iv) Computational Means

(a) Calendar Date

Calendar date for harvest is a reliable guide to commercial maturity for perennial fruit crops grown in seasonal climate which are more or less uniform from year to year. Time of flowering is largely dependent on temperature and the variation in number of days from flowering to harvest can be calculated for some commodities by use of degree day concept. Such harvesting criteria can be developed by growers based on their experiences.

(b) Heat Units

An objective measure of the time required for the development of the fruit to maturity after flowering can be made by measuring the degree days or heat units in a particular environment. It has been found that a characteristics number of heat unit or degree days are required to mature a crop under usually warm conditions, maturity will be advanced and under cooler conditions, maturity is delayed. The number of degree days to maturity is determined over a period of several years by obtaining the algebraic sum from the differences, plus or minus, between the daily mean temperatures and a fixed base temperature (commonly the minimum temperature at which growth occurs). The average or characteristic number of degree-days is then used to forecast the probable date of maturity for the current year and as maturity approaches, it can be checked by other means.

(v) Physiological Methods

(a) Respiration Rate

In fruits, there are two respiratory patterns. One group has highest respiration rate is called non-climacteric fruits. The other group, called climacteric fruits, exhibit a temporary respiratory increase which occurs when the fruit reaches full maturation and size and is entering the ripening stage.

(b) Ethylene Evolution Rate

Climacteric fruits respond to ethylene differently than non-climacteric fruits. In climacteric fruits, the respiration climacteric and subsequent ripening and senescence are associated with a coincident increase in endogenous ethylene production. Ethylene applied exogenously to climacteric fruits can also produce the same response, depending on fruit species and its stage of maturity. Conversely, in non-climacteric fruits, increasing the exogenous ethylene concentration increases the respiration and senescence rate but both rates decline if ethylene is removed.

(vi) Light Transmittance Techniques

Light transmission properties are also used to measure the degree of maturity of fruits. Colour intensity, wavelength and brightness *etc.*, are measured and maturity is decided on the basis. These methods are based on the chlorophyll content of the fruit, which is reduced during maturation. The fruit is exposed to a bright light which is then switched off so that the fruit is in total darkness. Next a sensor measures the amount of light emitted from the fruit which is proportional to its chlorophyll content and thus its maturity.

Chapter 8

Biochemical Changes during Fruit Ripening

Ripening is the final stage of development of a fruit, which involves series of physiological and biochemical events leading to changes in colour, flavour, aroma and texture that make them both, attractive and tasty. It imparts numerous quality and nutritional characteristics to fruits, a significant component of the human diet. Texture changes during ripening help in determing the shelf life of a fruit and softening during ripening is associated with biochemical changes in cell wall. Fruit ripening is a genetically programmed stage of development overlapping with senescence. The fruit is said to be ripe when it attains full flavour and aroma and other characteristics of the best fruit of that particular cultivar. In climacteric fruits, mature fruit will require a ripening period before attaining a desirable stage of edibility. The sudden increase in the rate of respiration and autocatalytic production of ethylene result in a series of complex changes in the colour, sugar, acidity, texture and aroma volatiles that are crucial for the sensory quality. The most striking chemical changes which occur during the course of fruit ripening are modification in structure and composition of cell wall polysaccharides, starch hydrolysis, degradation of chlorophyll, production of carotenoid, anthocyanin and phenolic substances, accumulation of sugar and organic acid which are described below:

Cell Wall Changes

Cell wall consists of pectic substances and cellulose as the main components along with small amounts of hemicelluloses and non-cellulose polysaccharides. In cell wall, the changes particularly in the middle lamella which is rich in pectic polysaccharides are degraded, solubilised and softened during ripening which results into a loss of neutral sugars and acidic pectin (rhamnogalacturonan) of all cell wall. The soluble proportion of these polyuronides may increase to just double at the time of fruit ripening. The major enzymes implicated in the softening of fruits are pectinesterase, polygalacturonase, cellulose and β–galactosidase. Polygalacturonase and cellulose activities of the fruit tissues increased markedly during ripening in mango, guava and strawberry fruits. Both polygalacturonase and cellulose were absent or present at only a low level in the green date but displayed large increases in activity during ripening. The changes in polygalacturonase and cellulose activity were reflected in a reduction in fruit firmness and a decrease in anhydrogalacturonic acid (AGA) and cellulose content during ripening. Pectinesterase (PE) activity decrease in mango, guava and strawberry fruits during ripening but its activity was increased in date during ripening, although the degree of esterification (DE) of pectin decresed. Pectic substances in the cell of the fruit are cemented with protopectin found in primary wall responsible for firmness of fruits which later hydrolysed to pectin at ripening and then to pectic acid during senescence.

Starch and Sugars

During fruit ripening sugars levels within fruit tend to increase. With the advancement of maturity, the accumulated starch is hydrolysed into sugars (glucose, fructose or sugars) which is known as characteristics event for fruit ripening. A regular increase in the level of sugars in pear throughout the period of fruit development has been observed due to translocation of photosynthates from leaves to the young fruit which are partly used for synthesis of pectic substances and other cell wall materials and partly converted to the usual storage product, the starch. Further breakdown of sucrose into glucose and fructose are probably mediated by the action of invertase. Low levels of invertase activity have been linked to sucrose accumulation trait. Following are the predominant sugars of various fruits which are increased at ripening due to starch breakdown.

- **(i) Glucose:** Grape, date, fig, mulberry and strawberry.
- **(ii) Fructose:** Pear, pomegranate, apple and grape.
- **(iii) Sucrose:** mango, pineapple, banana, peach and apricot.

Organic Acid

In most of the fruits, the levels of organic acid decreases as the ripening progresses except in banana where malic acid increases by 1-5 per cent. There is decreased in total organic acid (malic, citric, quinic) in peach with the ripening of fruits, coinciding with deceasing titratable acidity. Being a major respiratory substrate, organic acid (predominating) is metabolized to a greater extent than the others and may fall by 50 per cent during the life of the fruit. The decline in the content of organic acids during fruit ripening might be due the result of an increase in membrane permeability which allowed acids to be stored in the respiring cells. Following are the dominant organic acids found in various fruits.

- **(i) Citric acid:** Citrus fruits, guava, mango, pineapple, pomegranate, Indian gooseberry, strawberry, fig.
- **(ii) Malic acid:** Apple, pear, peach, plum, apricot, cherry, banana, sweet lime.
- **(iii) Tartaric acid:** Grape and tamarind.

Pigments (Colour Compound)

The green colour of unripe fruit is largely due to the presence of chlorophylls and the development of different colours during ripening is due to the disappearance of these pigments and the synthesis of carotenoids. Anthocyanins which are localized within the vacuole are derived from the flavanoid compounds and as such are synthesized from the aromatic amino acids phenylalanine, also make a contribution to colours in some ripe fruits. They give rise to a wide range to of colour from red to blue. The chloroplasts in green immature fruit generally lose chlorophyll on ripening and change into chromoplasts which contain carotenoid pigments. Carotenoids are normally synthesized in green plant tissue a major product being β-carotene. However, in many fruits additional β-carotene and lycopene are synthesized during ripening. During the biosynthesis of carotenoids lycopene acts as the precursor of β-carotene. Similarly the red colour development in apples and purple colour development in grapes are due to the formation of anthocyanin pigments in their skin. Sometimes both types of pigments can occur in the same fruit. Following are the important pigments found in fruits:

- **(i) Chlorophyll:** Responsible for green colour which is decreased during ripening due to degradation by the enzyme chlorophyllase.
- **(ii) Carotenoids:** Increased during ripening such as
  - **(a) Carotene:** Imparts yellow or orange colour in the fruits mango, peach, papaya.
  - **(b) Xanthophyll:** Imparts yellow colour in the citrus fruits.
  - **(c) Lycopene:** Imparts red or pink colour in guava and grape.
  - **(d) Anthocyanin:** Responsible for red, blue and purple colour in the fruits *viz.*, apple, plum, phalsa, jamun, fig, pomegranate.

Phenolic Compounds

The Phjenolic compounds occur in all fruits as a diverse group of secondary metabolites. The phenolic content of most fruits decline from high levels during early growth to low levels when the fruit is considered to be physiologically mature and thereafter susceptible to the induction of ripening. Possibly the presence of higher concentrations of phenolics during early stages of development provide a protection mechanism to the phytohormones like auxin, gibberellins and cytokinin which play an important role in cell division and cell enlargement. The important group of enzymes responsible for the metabolism of phenolics is the polyphenol oxidases (PPO) which are of two types: Catechol oxidase and Laccase which catalyses the oxireduction of O-diphenols or P-diphenols, respectively and have been classified together under the general nature of monophenol mono oxygenases. The dominant phenolic compounds of various fruits are:

I. Cinnamic Acid Derivatives

These are decreased during ripening.

(i) Chlorogenic acid: Apple and peach.

(ii) P-coumaric acid: Grape, pineapple.
(iii) Cafeic acid: Grape
(iv) Dopamine: Banana (increased).

II. Flavans

Imparts astringency which is decreased during ripening.

(i) Catechin: Apple, peach, pear, plum.

III. Flavonols

These are also decreased during ripening.

(i) Quercitin-3-galactoside: Apple.
(ii) Quercitin-3-arabinoside: Plum.
(iii) Quercitin-3-glucoside: Stawberry.
(iv) Kaemerol-3-glucoside: Grape.
(v) Isorhametin-3-glucoside: Pear.
(vi) Myricetin-3-arabinoside: Craneberry.

IV. Flavones

Decreased during ripening.

(i) Nobiletin: Orange.
(ii) Tangeretin: Tangerines.

V. Flavanones

Decreased during ripening.

(i) Naringine: Grapefruit.
(ii) Hesperidin: Orange and lemon.

VI. Anthocyanins

These increased during ripening. Important anthocyanins of various fruits are:

(i) Cynidin-3-galactoside: Apple.
(ii) Cynidin-3-glucoside: Plum.
(iii) Cynidin-3-monoglucoside: Grape and fig.
(iv) Delphinidin 3,5 diglucoside: Pomegranate.
(v) Pelargonidin-3-glucoside: Strawberry
(vi) Malvidin-3-monoglucoside: Grape.

Flavouring or Colatile Compounds

Characteristics flavour of an individual fruit is derived from the production of specific flavouring volatile. These compounds are mainly esters, alcohols, aldehydes, acids and ketones which are increased during ripening. At least 230 and 330 different compounds in apple and orange fruits have been indicated. These compounds are usually present in fruits at very low levels oftenly as ppm. In apple, the threshold concentration of ethyl-2-methyl buyrate (an aromatic compound) was detected to be 0.001 µl/l. Following are the important volatile compounds found in various fruits:

(i) **Isopentylacetate** (ester): Banana.

(ii) **Cinanamyl acetate** (ester): Guava.

(iii) **Ethyl-2-methyl butyrate** (ester): Apple.

(iv) **Methyl anthralinate** (ester): Grape (*Vitis labrasca*).

(v) **Methyl and ethyl** (ester): Pear.

(vi) **Ethyl acetate** (ester): Pineapple.

(vii) **Geranol** (alcohol): Grape (*Vitis vinifera*).

(viii) **Linalool** (alcohol): Papaya and *Vitis vinifera.*

(ix) **Lactones** (alcohol): Peach

(x) **Limonene** (Hydrocarbon): Orange, mandarin, lemon, grapefruit.

Vitamins

The most important vitamin in fruits for human nutrition is vitamin C. More than 90 per cent of the vitamin C in human diets is supplied by fruits. L-ascorbic acid (Vitamin C) is the naturally occurring ascorbic acid in fruits. An increase in ascorbic acid content with the increase in fruit growth has been observed in pear and thereafter, the levels declined with the advancement of maturity and onset of fruit ripening. Besides, Vitamin C, some other vitamins like vitamin A, vitamin B are also found in significant quantities. Following are important vitamins present in various fruits:

(i) **Vitamin A (carotene):** Mango, papaya, jackfruit, date, fig. It increases during ripening.

(ii) **Vitamin B (Thiamine):** Grape. It increases during ripening.

(iii) **Vitamin B_2 (riboflavin):** Bael, Pineapple, Papaya. It increases during ripening.

(iv) **Vitamin C (ascorbic acid):** Guava, Aonla, citrus fruits. It decreases in most of fruits at ripening.

Amino Acids

Amino acid are known as the building blocks of proteins. These are to be metabolic equilibrium with the process of photosynthesis and degradation. Generally in most of the fruits, a declining trend was observed in the contents of amino acid as they approach of maturity. The sharp decrease in free amino acids towards maturity and onset of ripening has been attributed to their incorporation into protein required for the synthesis of various ripening enzymes. Among the 14 free amino acids detected in apple fruit, isoleucine which is considered to be the biosynthetic precursor of some branched chain estrs showed a great increase during fruit ripening while the others decreased or remained stable. Similarly, the main amino acids in young Barlett pear fruit were reported as asparagines (57 per cent), aspartic acid (17 per cent) and glumatic acid (8 per cent). Dominant amino acids of various fruits which increased during fruit ripening are:

(i) **Alanine:** Mango, goose berry, date.

(ii) **Arginine:** Grape.

(iii) **Proline:** Grape, pear, orange.

(iv) **Aspartic acid:** Apple, pear, banana, grapefruit, lemon.

(v) **Isoleucine:** Apple, banana, breadfruit.

(vi) **Methionine:** Pineapple.

(vii) **Histidine:** Banana.

Lysine and proline in mango and glutamic acid in banana decreased during ripening.

Proteins and Enzymes

The amount of proteins in apple varies with the stage of maturity. An increase in protein synthesis during early climacteric period has been observed in many fruits. During ripening of apple and pear, there is a net increase of protein nitrogen and malic enzyme. Evidences showed that proteins were synthesized by the action of enzymes during ripening. Enzymes of various fruits which increased during fruit ripening are:

(i) **Amylase** (Starch hydrolysis): Banana and mango.

(ii) **Chlorophyllase** (Chlorophyll degradation): Apple, citrus, banana.

(iii) **Invertase** (Sucrose hydrolysis): Banana.

(iv) **Malic enzyme** (malic acid degradation): Grape

(v) **Pectin esterase** (cell wall degradation): Banana, citrus, mango,pear, apple and peach.

(vi) **Peroxidase** (Ethylene synthesis): Mango.

(vii) **Fatty acid synthetase** (Fatty acid synthesis): Avocado.

(viii) **Polygalacturonase** (middle lamella dessolvation): Softening in many fruits.

(ix) **Polyphenol oxidase** (Phenol oxidation): Apple, banana.

(x) **Phosphatase** (Phosphoric acid hydrolysis): Mango and apple.

(xi) **Ribonuclease** (RNA degradation): Apple.

Hormones

Ethylene has long been regarded as the main regulator of ripening in climacteric fruits. The ethylene concept of fruit ripening is due to its evolution during ripening and its exogenous application. Ethylene increases enzyme activity and cell membrane permeability which involve an increase in respiration and leading to ripening. Ethylene and abscisic acid increased during ripening of fruits while GA, auxins and cytokinins decreased during ripening.

Fatty Acids

Peculiar flavour and aroma of some fruits exist due to the some fatty acids which increase during ripening. Dominant fatty acids of various fruits are as follows:

(i) **Palmitic acid:** Avocado, mango, almond

(ii) **Palmitoleic acid:** Mango

(iii) **Oleic acid:** Avocado

(iv) **Linoleic acid:** Mahua

(v) **Stearic acid:** Banana

The ratio of palmitic and palmitoleic acid determines the flavour and aroma of mango. If it is less than 1 (0.8-0.9) then a strong flavour and aroma occurs in the varieties Alphonso and Langra while it is more than 1 (1.1-1.5) then less aroma and flavour occurs in Neelam and Banglora varieties of mango.

Minerals

There is little change in mineral content of fruit at ripening. Potassium and sodium increase and calcium decreases during ripening.

Chapter 9

Ethylene Management in Fruits

Ethylene in Fruit Ripening

Production and Effects

As back as 1910 British colonies were there in several continents. They import fruit and vegetable from different continents. Jamaica to Europe – The banana which changing colour when kept with green banana, peaches and nursery stock, there was some substance which cause banana, green mature peaches to ripe and damage the nursery stock. Even the Chinese know that there is somje gas which causes pears to ripe and this gas is emmited by smokes of incense (Chorchort) in close rooms. This was identified as ethylene gas (C_2H_4) in 1934. It has been a practices in California and Florida, to use this gas for degreening of oranges and other citrus fruits. This gas was produced from kerosene fuels and axaust of .... Denny (1924) proved that ethylene was active degreening agent in stove gas and that its low conc. of 5 ppm degreens lemon in 6-8 days time. Today so many reviews are available an ethylene including Spencer (1965), Hansen (1966), Prath and Goeschel (1969), Mc-Glasson (1970). Ables (1973), Morris and Liebermaun (1979) and Dilley (1982). They deal role of ethylene in fruit ripening and mechanism in physiological processes. Ethylene was also used for blunching of celavy and ripening of many fruits. Now it is used commercially for ripening of banana. Honeydew Melons, Tomatoes and degreening of citrus fruits. Ables (1972) found that it was found in all the organs and tissues of the palnt after measurement. Burg (1972) found in 90 plants, flower, leafy stem, roots and seeds including the fungus *Penicillium degitatium* in which ethylene was identified. Only low conc. of ethylene was required to produce physiol. Effect. Ex. Pear seedling grown in dark, sensitive to 0.025-0.1 ppm of ethylene and are used for bioassay method for ethylene. As little as 0.5 ppm ethylene will injure the carnation and there buds will not open. Because of its effect on growth and ripening this has been considered as plant hormone.

Advances in Methodology

In begening there are no appropriate method which can detect the ethylene in various parts. This was until the development of Gas Chrom, it was believed that only climacteric frits produce ethylene gas. When the manometric methods were used then some of the climacteric fruits did not even show its (ethylene) presence. Example Mango. Biale *et al.*, 1954 concluded that a fruit with a certain ripening and respiratory behavior is not a ipsofacto a ethylene producer. The mango has a pronounced climacteriv but no ethylene could be detected. It was only in 1957 when Mukherjee and Snock, observed that vapor given off by ripening mangoes caused the premature mangoes to ripen and this gave clear indication that ethylene was produced by ripening mangoes. Mukherjee (1960) confirmed the evolution of ethylene by mangoes during ripening using biological and chemical tests.

Mattoo *et al.*, 1968 determined ethylene concentration in the gases which evolved from ripening. Alphonso mango slices by using chromatogric telh. and reported that conc. of ethylene range from 0.02-0.18 ppm. These reports confirmed that mango do produce ethyelene during ripening. Mango varieties showed enough internal accumulation of ethylene which resulted the ripening at or just before begening of respiratory climacteric. This has been confirmed that ethylene is an essential hormone for process of ripening. Now how essential is ethylene for ripening. This can be made clear if we an able to show that (i) the process of ripening will not be initiated if ethylene is totally absent. (ii) If it can be demonstrated that no other substance can duplicate the action of ethylene on ripening process (3) if the immediate respiratory response is obtained by exogenous ethylene application. The test were conducted on these lines but unfortunately there is no method which can detect the ethylene content completely gases have been found which cause fruits to ripen but they are not as effective as ethylene. (4) That if we are able to demonstrate that ethylene is necessary for various process of ripening. (5) If you are able to demonstrate that ethylene production occur just before onset of climacteric. (6) The internal conc. of ethylene before the climacteric ascent is physiologically active.

Conclusions

(1) Ethylene continuously produced as a metabolic product and is dissolved in cytoplasm or absorved in organells. (2) Why it is true the ethylene inhances respiration, its formation is inhanced only active respiration hence arose the idea of autocatalytic action of ethylene. (3) The ratio of respiration to ethylene is not constant as fruits ripen, the ethylene content drops off. (4) It is not known whether ethylene is required throughout the ripening process.

Effects

These are very important to us for postharvest physiology because it cause the ripening of fruits and vegetables. It was recorded that atleast 1 ppm ethylene is required to bring about ripening and conc. even less than 1 ppm is equally effective depending upon the type, variety and temperature condition of fruits. If the fruits are not reached the premature stage the fruits will not ract with the ethylene even it is exogenously applied. In many cases green tissues have turned yellow but that does not mean the ripening has been completed. This shows ripening process comes at certain physiological age. Once the process of ripening is started, it is irreversible. In case of fleshy fruits although respiration rate increased during ripening the respiration is not the cause of ripening but it is rather the by product of all changes in texture, colour and chemical transformation that are going on in the fruits. The amount of ethylene required in the tissues of the fruit to initiate various ripening reactions differ force. About 10 times as much ethylene was required top induce pigment change in honeydew melons as to induce softening. Ethylene is known induce to chlorophilase activitiy and senesance and the primary role of ethylene in the digreening process is the dissumption of chloroplast membrance (Pruvis, 1979).

Controlled Atmosphere Storage

The conc. of various gases particularly CO_2 and O_2 can be regulated. The effects of ethylene can be very much minimized at the temperature 32° – 34°F. But if the storage commodity is very sensitive, this temperature will affect Ex. nursh-7 plants. When the temperature is 95°F, neither there will be production of ethylene nor will any effect if applied from outside. Lieberman and Mapson (1964) Effect of ethylene can be inhibited by ethylene acide. Other chemicals which are used for delaying sensence like Alar, Bg (SADH). When there chemicals are used for delaying the senescence, they inhibit the ethylene production and its effect. Some fruits ex. Avocado, Mangoes and Apple they will not ripen properly if they remain on the tree and it has been suggested that unripening on the tree is due to certain ethylene inhibitor produced by leaves. The effect of growth regulator on fruit ripening show that they induce ethylene production. Ex. Fig 2, 4, 5-T bring about incaused ethylene production. Similarly whatever chemicals are used for thinning of fruits and when the chemical harvesting is practiced, there effect is also the induction of ethylene. The most important ethylene production chemical is 2- chloroethyl phosphoric Acid (Ethepon, Ethrel, CEPA, Amchem-66-3294). This breaks down when applied, releases ethylene. This bring about disease and freez resistant besides other beneficial effect. Some determental effects premature ripening, lethal damage to nursery stock, Petal fall and failure of buds to open flower, Russet spotting in lettuce (1 ppm or less ethylene exposure), bitterness in carrots and skin injury and incuase decay susceptibility in citrus fruits. Since ethylene is produced in fleshy fruits when ripening, therefore, it is advisable there fruits are never stored along with the leafy vegetable, Nursery stock *etc.* in storage. It is also advisable to bring down the temperatore to reuce its effect. In case the storage space limited and necessary to store few things together, store the commodity at 32°-34°F and increase the free ventilation. If you increase ventilation in cold storage, there will be rapid loss of refrigeration. In such ventilation the filters are kept towards the air is entering. There filters are kept with Purafel. In the absence of Purafel and Brominated activated charcoal can be kept. But in this case one more precantion is to be taken, you will have to provide a layer of non activated and non brominated charcoal so that bromine can not pass through. Regarding storage apple at 32°F, they found to contain 2-40 ppm ethylene. Golden delicious produce maximum amount of ethylene during storage. Under controlled atmosphere of apple at 37°F and pear at 34°F, the ethylene production begin after 20 days and thereafter it increase at peak conc. of

100-150 ppm and this peak is maintained for many months and the highest value was recorded as 600 ppm without damage of Apple and pears. The highest value was recorded in golden delicious at 3.5°C when CO_2 conc. 0.5 per cent and O_2 was 2 per cent, ethylene conc. was 2300 ppm (0.24 per cent). Even at such high conc. it does not cause ripening. When the temperature was increased as 54°F, then there was striking effect of ethylene varies internal conc. of ethylene 0.05 ppm (Gross Michal Banana) – 2500 ppm (Boldwins and Mac-Intosh apple).

This is dependant (internal conc.) on two factor:

1. Production rate of tissue.
2. Defusion of gases from the tissue.

They effect the surface to mass ratio.

Dense tissue with inter cellular spaces Ex. Potato.

Rate of CO_2 production is much more than ratio of ethylene. Apple 50 µ lit./hr., the ratio of CO_2 production to ethylene at room temperature is about 300:1. Ethylene is believed to produced in all enzymatically by methionine which is an amino acid. Site of action of ethylene in side the cell is not very clear. Ethylene is said to effect membrance permeability and permeability of all the respirating wall inside the cell. So far as the ethylene is found in side the cell in mobile form. CO_2 is another important gas which compete with ethylene at the site of action and therefore, this becomes an important point which prevents the biological response to ethylene. The effects of low origen conc. in retarding in ripening are believed to the due to the inhibition of ethylene production and action and are not dependant an respiration inhibition. O_2 may be attached to a receiptor or indirectly oxidate before ethylene can react.

Mechanism of Ethylene Action in Ripening

There is no evidence at present to say that ethylene is a part of any reaction or act as co-enzyme of co-factor at the cellular level, ethylene is believed to increase the permeability of cell membrane and inner membranes thus making the substract more accessible to the corresponding enzymes as has been reported by Provis (1979). In the degreening process of citrus ethyle known to induce chlorophyllase activity. The role chlorophyllase in chlorophyll degradation in doubtful because the high levels of chlorophyllase activity is observed at the time other than sensense. The ethyle involved the disumption of chlorophyll membrane Ethylene is easily soluble in lipids and in of the experimental cases, ethylene have not been found to broud stage at any site. Terai *et al.* (1972) demonstrated that how ethylene is movile. He took Banana, after 3 hrs. at distal end of the fruit start emitting ethylene. CO_2 evolution took 18 hrs. in same case.

Mattoo and Modi (1969) have shown that C_2H_4 promoted the activities of the enzymes catalase, peroreidase and amylase in the slices prepared from low-climacteric mango. During this stimulation the respective protainaceous ripening inhibitor disappear within 45 hrs. in the treated slices. Ethylene treatment resulted in the softening of slices and appreciable change in colour from white to yellow and thereby suggesting the symptoms which aer characteristic of ripening. The role of ethylene, the ethylene can inactivate the partially purified preparations in hibitors with respect of catalase and perorcidase because the treated preparations did not show any inhibitory action of these enzymes. On the basis of above otoser. They suggested 3 things (1) Before the onset of climacteric in mangoes, ethylene synthesize by the fruit stimulates the oxidative and hydrolytic enzymes and inactivates the inhibitors of these enzymes. (2) After during this process solubilization of isoluble cellular components takes place leading to changes in the cellular permeability and thus allowing for more interaction of the fruit substracts with their enzyme. (3) All these processes together with other hitterto unknown factors vigously initiate a part of metabolic system eventually resulting the ripening of fruits.

Table 9

Conc. of Ethylene ppm	Peronidase Activity μ mol^{-1} mg^{-1} Protein				
	0 hr.	17th hrs.	24th hrs.	45th hrs.	70th hrs.
0	0.22	0.200	0.256	0.352	0.12
10	0.22	0.446	0.580	0.660	0.40
50	0.22	0.546	0.657	0.600	0.59

Synthesis and Biogenesis of Ethylene

Various theories have been formed suggesting the synthesis of ethylene. *Pencillium degitatum* is a good source of ethylene but the synthesis of ethylene in Pencillium is different than those of higher plants. These are 7 theories:

1. **Proposed by Mapson and Lieberman, 1964:** Known as Linolenate Scheme: non enzymatic scheme: In this immediate precurson is suppose to be Linolenic acid. This system requires cuprousion as catalyst.
2. **Ethanol pathway:** suggested by phan, 1963, explained by Shimokawa and Kasai (1966).
3. **β-alanine pathway:** Suggested by Thompson and Spencer (1967).
4. **Methionine pathway:** Developed by Matto and Modi (1967): finding was bored on mango. Methionine was told the immediate precursor for biogenesis of ethylene.
5. **Methionol intermediate:** Yang, 1968.
6. **Pyridoxal phosphate mediate methionis scheme:** Yang and Baur (1972).
7. **Peptide mediated methonine pathway:** Demases and Stahman (1971).
8. **Morris and Lieberman (1979):** Biosynthesis and action of ethylene. Anal. Pl. Physiol Vol 30: 553-91.

Intermediates of crab cycle are involved. In case of *Penecillium degitatum* methionine is not found but lot of ethylene is produced but in fruits L-methionine is involved. Tissues are more than precursors of ethylene. Methionine is the most important precursor.

The gaseous hormone ethylene has significance in the practical agriculture, basic biochemistry and physiology of plants have been studied for many decades. Elucidation of the ethylene biosynthetic pathway by Adams and Yang (1979) and the complexities of ethylene biosynthesis and action have stimulated research in this area. The ripening of climacteric fruits represents the unique co-ordination of developmental and biochemical pathways leading to the changes in colour, texture, aroma and nutritional quality of fruits. The gaseous plant hormone ethylene plays a key regulatory role in fruit ripening. Rapid ripening of climacteric fruits during storage causes about 15 per cent losses. The reason behind the losses during storage and postharvest is autocatalytic production of ethylene, which leads to loss of sensory properties of fruits and ultimately market value. Autocatalytic production of ethylene causes detrimental effects by increasing rate of respiration; accelerate senescence and chemical changes which affect postharvest life and quality of fruits. Various tools used for management of ethylene during postharvest stage are control atmospheric storage, modified atmospheric storage but it has its own limitations and most of the time leads to disorders like superficial scald, melting flesh and chilling injury.

Fruit ripening is defined as the integrated sequence of changes, including softening, change in colourand accumulation of sugars and aromatics, coupled with a decline in organic acids (Vendrell *et al.*, 2001). It is considered to begin during the later stages of fruit maturation and it transforms a fully grown mature but inedible plant organ into an attractive fruit to eat. While maturation and development are completed only when fruit are attached to the plant, ripening and senescence can proceed on or off the plant. Fruit are divided into two groups based on their ripening pattern: climacteric and non-climacteric fruit. In climacteric fruit, ripening is accompanied by a peak in respiration which coincides with a burst in ethylene production while ripening in non-climacteric fruit does not show a peak in respiration and ethylene production rates remain low. Some species show clear climacteric (*e.g.*, apple, tomato and banana) or non-climacteric (orange and pineapple) behavior while others (like melon) comprise both climacteric and non-climacteric genotypes (Pech *et al.*, 2008. Ethylene is the most prominent ripening regulating hormone. There are two systems involved in its biosynthesis, System-1 functions during vegetable growth, is auto inhibited by ethylene. This is responsible for the production of basal levels of ethylene synthesized by plant tissues, including non-climacteric fruit. System-2 comes into play during the ripening of climacteric fruit and is characterized by an autocatalytic ethylene (McMurchie *et al.*, 1972). The main difference between system-1 and system-2 is the negative and respectively positive feedback regulation of ethylene.

Softening is for the major part regulated by ethylene, as is abscission, chlorophyll degradation, aroma volaties production and climacteric respiration and ethylene production. The climacteric ethylene production is triggered by an ethylene independent process. The different ethylene dependent processes can differ strongly in sensitivity levels to ethylene and internal production of ethylene (Flores *et al.*, 2001). The higher ethylene production also have some detrimental effect like accelerates senescence, enhances excessive softening of fruits, promotes discolouration, stimulates phenylpropanoid metabolism, stimulates chlorophyll loss and induces many physiological disorders during storage.

Table 10: Postharvest Losses of Major Fruits in India during 2010 and 2015

Sl.No.	*Name of Fruits*	*Per cent Average Loss (CIPHT, Nanda et al., 2010)*	*Per cent Average Loss (CIPHT, Jha et al., 2015)*
1	Apple	12.26	10.39
2	Banana	6.60	7.76
3	Citrus	6.38	9.69
4	Grapes	8.30	8.63
5	Guava	18.05	15.88
6	Mango	12.74	9.16
7	Papaya	7.36	6.70
8	Sapota	5.77	9.73

Source: Hort. Stat., Ministry of Agriculture, India 2015.

Inhibitors of Ethylene Action

Most of the effects of ethylene can be antagonized by specific ethylene inhibitors. Silver ions (Ag+) applied as silver nitrate (AgNO3) or as silver thiosulfate (Ag(S203)2^{3-}) are potent inhibitors of ethyelen action. Carbon dioxide at high concentrations (in the range of 5 to 10 per cent) also inhibits many effects of ethylene, such as the induction of fruit ripening, although CO_2 is less efficient than Ag+. This effect of CO_2 has often been exploited in the storage of fruits whose ripening is delayed at elevated CO_2 concentrations. The volatile compound *trans*-cyclooctene, is a strong competitive inhibitor of ethylene binding to the receptor.

1-methylecyclopropene

The 1-MCP is competitive inhibitor of ethylene action used to maintain fruit quality by delaying senescence. It is a gaseous chemical that can be easily applied. The 1-MCP has non toxic mode of action and activity at very low concentration increases its commercial importance. It binds irreversibly to the ethylene receptor and inhibits further processes that are controlled by ethylene. The 1-MCP is registered by more than 37 countries for use in apple, peach, plu, pear, mango, banana, papaya and so on after approval by Environmental Protection Agency of USA. A treated fruit have lowered ethylene production, slow rate of respiration and maintained physiochemical properties during both ambient and cold storage. The response of 1-MCP typically dependent on concentration and exposure time. Various genotypes, cultivars and maturity stage at time of treatment give varying response to the 1-MCP. 1-Methylcyclopropene (1-MCP) is an inhibitor of ethylene perception, has been commercialized as SmartFresh™ technology for postharvest use on fruits and vegetables around the world. 1-MCP is used widely on apple fruit in North America; its successful commercial uptake has occurred because the technology helps to maintain quality of the fruit, non only during storage but also through the entire marketing chain inclouding the consumers' homes. 1-MCP can reduce a number of serious storage disorders that cause fruit loss, such as senescent breakdown and superficial scald but the incidence of others including carbon dioxide injury and flesh browning, can be increased by 1-MCP. Blankenship *et al.* (2003) reviewed that the 1-MCP prevents effects of ethylene in a wider range of fruits, vegetables and floriculture crops. The low concentrations are effective and ranges from 2.5 nlL^{-1} to 1 ml L^{-1}. The interaction of concentration with temperature such that low concentrations of 1-MCP applied over longer durations may be as effective as high concentrations. 1-MCP is most commonly applied at 20-25°C, also can be used at lower temperatures in some commodities. Generally, treatment durations of 12-24 h were sufficient to achieve a full response. The various factors required to be considered at time of using 1-MCP including cultivar, developmental stage, time from harvest to treatment and multiple applications. Depending on the species being treated, 1-MCP shows a variety of effects on respiration, ethylene production, volatile production, chlorophyll degradation and other colour changes, protein and membrane changes, softening, disorders and diseases, acidity and sugars.

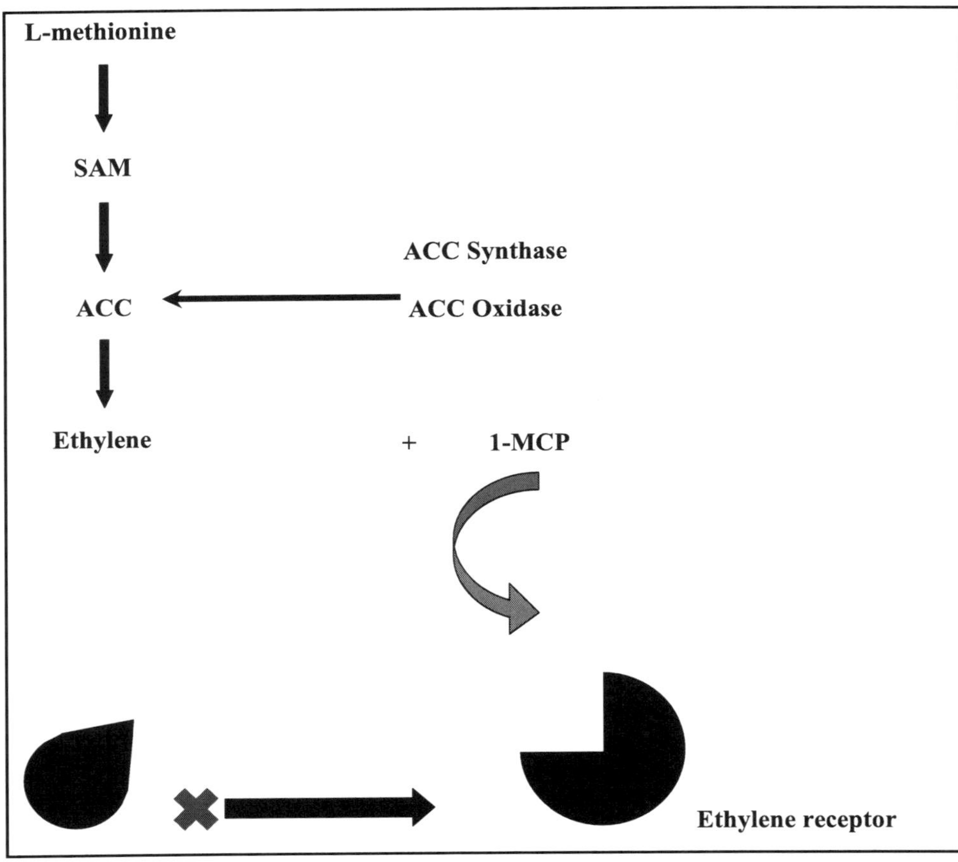

Figure 3: Mode of Action of 1-MCP.

Table 10: Recommendations for Use of 1-MCP in Important Fruit Crops

Fruits	*Concentrations*	*Treatment Temperature (ºC)*	*Treatment Time*	*Effects*	*Reference*
Apple	0.6-2 ml/L	0, 5, 10, 15, 20, 25	7-20 hour	Maintained firmness, maintain titratable acidity, reduced vilatiles, slowed loss of chlorophyll and starch, inhibited ethylene, reduced respiration and decay, prevented disorders like superficial scald.	Watkins *et al.* (2000), DeEll *et al.* (2016), Miho *et al.* (2006), Lum *et al.* (2016), Susan Lurie, 2007.
	937 nL/L	15-17	20-21 hour	The treatment of 'Granny Smith' apples with 1-MCP can extend the storage (0-1 ºC, 90-95 per cent RH) time for 3 months without significantly losing freshness even two weeks after removal from cold storage. It is more effective in preserving sensory attributes related to apple freshness when compared with the DPA (diphenylamine) treatment.	Tomic *et al.* (2016)
Banana	5-500 nl/L, 0.1 ml/L	20, 24	6-24 hour	Delayed ripening and peel colour change.	Harris *et al.* (2000), Golding *et al.* (1998)
Banana	50 mL L^{-1} ethephon with 400 nL L^{-1} 1-MCP	20, 24	16 hour	Improper concentration of 1-MCP and treatment time affect vital components of banana fruit quality. The treatment affect rate of respiration and ethylene production. The 1-MCP reduces the activity of pectin lyase, pectin methylesterase, cellulose and Polygalactouronase and delayed the peak activity of ACC synthase and ACC oxidase. The combined treatment significantly delayed the formation of volatile compounds, ripening of fruits which ultimately prolonged the post harvest life of banana without affecting its normal coloring and volatile development which maintained the marketability of banana fruit.	Zhu *et al.* (2015)
Papaya	50-1000 nL/L	22	5-24 hour	Reduces rate of respiration and ethylene production, maintain firmness and texture.	Manenoi *et al.* (2007)
Sapota	300 nL/L	25	12 hour	Delayed softening, Inhibition of cell wall degrading enzymes	Moris *et al.* (2008)

Fruits	*Concentrations*	*Treatment Temperature (ºC)*	*Treatment Time*	*Effects*	*Reference*
Plum	1, 13, 26 or 39 ml/L	20	6, 20, 24 hour	Reduced ethylene and respiration, maintained firmness, slowed colour change, decreased internal flesh browning	Abdi *et al.* (1998)
Plum (*Prunus salicina* Lindl.) cv. Tegan Blue	0, 0.5, 1.0 or 2.0 μLL^{-1}	20±1	24 hour	Fruit were allowed to ripen at ambient temperature (20±1 ºC). The reducing activities of ethylene biosynthesis enzymes ACS, ACO and ACC content with postharvest treatments of 1-MCP. The reduction in fruit softening enzymes (PE, EGase, exo-PG and endo-PG) in fruit skin and in pulp tissues were more pronounced with increased concentrations of 1-MCP.	Khan *et al.* (2007)
Peach	20 nL/L, 0.1 ml/L, 0.5 ml/L	20-24 hour	4, 18, 24 hour	Maintained firmness, delayed ethylene production and reduced activity of ethylene associated enzymes.	Fan *et al.* (2002), Liguori *et al.* (2004)
Pineapple	0.1 ppm (4.5 nmol 1^{-1})	20	18 hour	Effectively controlled internal browning, a chilling injury symptom, in pineapples stored at 10ºC for 4 weeks. Delayed ascorbic acid decline and arrested the decline in both total soluble solids and ethylene synthesis. 1-MCP could be considered for use commercially to control this important postharvest physiological disorder in pineapples.	Selvarajah, S. *et al.* (2001)

The 1-methylcyclopropene was a potent inhibitor of ripening of mango cv. Alphonso. It can increases shelf life of fruits by retarding biochemical changes and enhancing shelf life of fruits without losing quality during cold storage. The analysis for chemical as well as sensory properties of Alphonso mango fruits under cold storage indicated that Cel-fresh 0.18 per cent Tablet (1-MCP)-1 Tablet/2M3 treatment (T2) was superior over control and better than other treatments (Sonune *et al.*, 2015). The 1-MCP treatment leds to decreased levels of H_2O_2 and lipid peroxidation, concomitant with increased activities and isozymes of catalase (CAT) and superoxide dismutase (SOD). Whereas the ethrel treatment causes an increase in H_2O_2 and lipid peroxidation, concomitant with a decrease in the activities and isozymes of catalase and SOD. Guaiacol peroxidase (GPS) was not detected in both control and treated fruits. The treatment of ethylene increases activity of ascorbate peroxidase (APX) while 1-MCP treatment only increase in marginal APX (Singh *et al.*, 2008).

Ripening of mango fruit is characterized by softening of flesh which limits its shelf life. 1-MCP is nontoxic gas that delays fruit softening and improves quality of several fruit. The role of 1-MCP in regulating fruit softening and quality of 'Kensington Pride' mango was investigated by treating physiological mature fruits treated with 1-MCP (1 mL L^{-1}), ethylene (10 mL L^{-1}) or 1-MCP + ethylene for 12 hour at ambient condition (20 ± 1 °C). Fruits were allowed to ripe at ambient temperature (20 ± 1 °C) for 10 days. Climacteric peaks of ethylene production and respiration rate were significantly suppressed by 1-MCP application as compared to ethylene-treated and control fruits. Exogenous application of ethylene accelerated the development of fruit colour, fruit softening with increased activities of exo-Polygalacturonase, endo- Polygalacturonase and endo-1, 4-β-d-glucanase (EGase) enzymes in the pulp tissues. Whereas, activities of fruit softening enzymes were significantly delayed and/or suppressed in 1-MCP-treated fruit. 1-MCP treated fruit showed improved rheological properties (*i.e.*, firmness, springiness and stiffness), decreased level of citric acid, malic acid, succinic acid, total organic acids, total sugars and sucrose than other treatments. 1-MCP inhibited the activities of fruit softening enzymes which consequently delayed the ripening and ripening related changes in 'Kensington Pride' mango (Razzaq *et al.*, 2016).

Tatsuki *et al.* (2007) studied expression patterns of genes for ethylene biosynthesis, enzymes and ethylene receptor in two apple cultivars, Orin and Fuji. Both cultivars responds in different manner but the ultimate storage life and firmness was improved by 1-MCP. Watkins *et al.* (2000) investigated the potential for commercial application of 1-methylcyclopropene (1-MCP) to maintain quality of 'McIntosh', 'Empire', 'Delicious' and 'Law Rome' (early, mid and late season) apples under air and controlled atmosphere (CA) storage conditions. These cultivars represent early, mid and late season apples with ripening rates ranging from fast to slow. 1-MCP gas concentrations used were 0.1, 1 and 2 ml/L, generated from Ethylbloc™ powder. Effects of 1-MCP were greater in CA than air storage. A dose response of internal ethylene concentrations and flesh firmness to 1-MCP was found in 'McIntosh' and 'Law Rome' but 'Delicious' and 'Empire' ripening was generally prevented by all 1-MCP concentrations. 1-MCP reduced superficial scald incidence and accumulations of a-farnesene and conjugated trienols during air storage. The results indicate that the efficacy of 1-MCP is affected by cultivars and storage conditions.

The losses due to compression during transport are heavy in the fruits like plum due to its delicate nature and requires massive postharvest managements for enhancing its shelf-life so as to make it available in the market for longer time. Sharma *et al.* (2013) studied the effect of 1-MCP treatment on Santa Rosa plum of two maturity groups (climacteric and pre-climacteric) during transportation. Plums of both maturity stages were subjected to 1-MCP treatments 1-MCP @ 1.5 $\mu l\ l^{-1}$ for 24 hour at 20°C, then packed in CFB boxes and transported by road. The losses were higher in climacteric stage (25.0 per cent) than pre-climacteric (9.0 per cent) stage, whereas, the 1-MCP (1.5 $\mu l\ l^{-1}$) treatments had significantly reduced compression injury, being the least (0.0). There was significant losses reported in quality parameters like fruit firmness, AOX capacity, TSS, acidity and ascorbic acid in untreated plums. Similarly, respiration and ethylene evolution rates were higher in untreated plums than those, which were treated with 1-MCP, being the least in treated fruits.

Interactions between control atmospheric storage and multiple treatments of 1-MCP showed that second application of 1-MCP after 4 months storage in CA may improve firmness (DeEll *et al.*, 2016). The treatment of 'Granny Smith' apple with 1-MCP can extend storage time without losing freshness and sensory properties even two weeks after removal from cold storage (Tomic *et al.*, 2016). Harris *et al.* (2000) reported that 1-MCP significantly delayed ripening of banana fruits over control which help in export of fruits.

Lohani *et al.* (2003) reported that activities of pectin methyl esterase (PME), polygalacturonase (PG), pectate lyase (PL) and cellulose in banana cv. Dwarf Cavendish fruit were measured over a period of 7 days after ripening was initiated with ethylene. Effects of treatments with 1-methylcyclopropene (1-MCP), abscisic acid (ABA) and indole acetic acid (IAA) on activities of these hydrolases were measured in order to help elucidate their roles during banana ripening. Ethylene stimulated activities of all four enzymes, at best differentially. 1-MCP and IAA suppressed the ethylene effects.

The papaya fruit treated with 1-MCP when more than 25 per cent ripe had a delay in softening. The 1-MCP maintained fruit firmness and texture that may have commercial utility (Manenoi *et al.*, 2007). Morais *et al.* (2008) investigated the influence of 1-methylcyclopropene (1-MCP) on the physiological and biochemical changes that sapodilla cell wall undergoes during ripening and evaluated its potential to preserve sapodilla fruits at postharvest. Fruits were treated with ethylene antagonist 1-MCP at 300 nL L^{-1} for 12 hour and then stored under a modified atmosphere at 25°C for 23 days. 1-MCP significantly delayed softening of sapodilla for 11 days as a consequence of inhibition of cell wall degrading enzyme activities and thus 1-MCP treated fruits exhibited a less extensive solubilisation of polyuronides, hemicelluloses and of free neutral sugar when compared to control fruit. Delayed softening of sapodilla is largely dependent on ethylene production and perception.

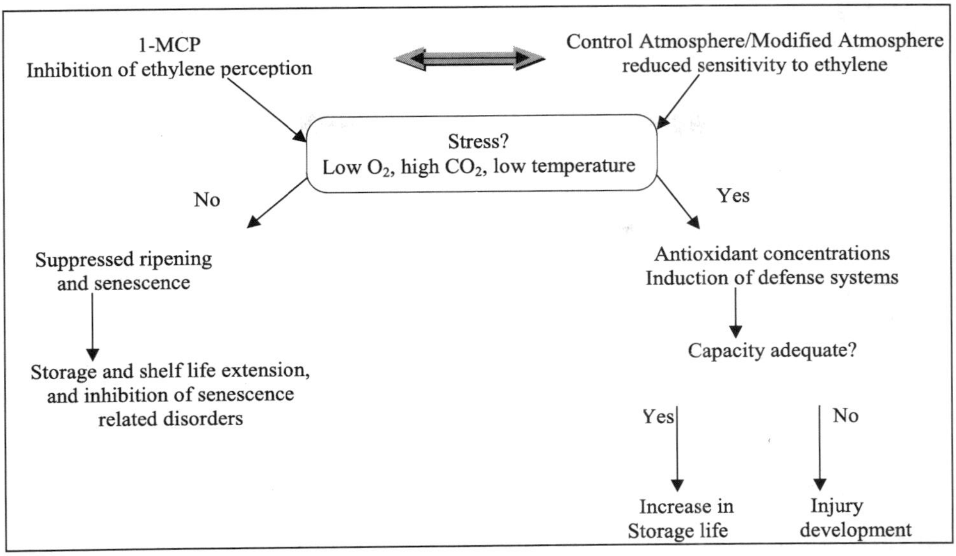

Figure 4: Proposed Interaction between 1-MCP, Stress and Storage Life or Injury.

The Nitric oxide (NO) discovered by Joseph Priestly (1772) and called it "Nitrous air". Wilson *et al.* (2008) reported the various routes of nitric oxide (NO) production in plants cells. NO can be synthesized enzymatically from nitrite (NO_2^-) by nitrate reductase (NR). There is also considerable evidence for 1-arginine-dependent NO synthase (NOS) activity in plant cells, although the protein at NOS1 is no longer considered to be a NOS and no other plant candidate for the role has been identified. Evidence also exists for the activity of a nitrite: NO reductase in roots and for the ability of both chloroplasts and mitochondria to convert NO_2^- to NO. Nitric Oxide is first gas known to act as a biological messenger and plays important role in inhibition of ethylene biosynthesis and its related detrimental effect on fruits during postharvest storage.

Monitoring ethylene is crucial in regulating postharvest life of fruits. The concept of nitric oxide (NO) involvement in regulating ethylene is new. NO mediated physiologies casted through regulation of plant hormones are widely reported during developmental and stress chemistry having no direct link with ripening. NO biology and understanding its interplay with other signal molecules in ripening fruits suggest ways of achieving greater synergies with nO applications. Experiments focused at convincingly demonstrating the involvement of NO in altering ripening-related ethylene profile of fruits, would help develop new processes for shelf life extension. The putative mechanisms of NO intricacies with other primary and secondary signals are hypothesized. The advantage of eliciting NO endogenously may open up various biotechnological opportunities for its precise delivery into the target tissues (Manjunath *et al.*, 2010).

Table 11: Various Routes of Nitric Oxide (NO) Production within Plant Cells

Pathways	*1*	*2*	*3*	*4*	*5*
Precursors	NO^-_2	NO^-_2	NO^-_2	NO^-_2	L-Arginine
Site of synthesis	Plasma membrane (root)	Cytoplasm	Mitochondria	Chloroplast	Cytoplasm Mitochondria Chloroplast
Enzymes	Nitrite NO reductase (Ni-NOR)	Nitrate reductase (NR)	-	-	AtNOS1 AtNOA1

Table 12: Application of NO for Shelf Life Extension

Fruits	*Treatment*	*Extent of Shelf Life Extension (Per cent)*	*Specific conditions*	*Reference*
Kiwi	NO gas	160	Not specified	Leshem *et al.* (1998)
Strawberry	NO gas in the concentration range 5-10 ml 1^{-1}	>50	No significance of storage temperature	Wills *et al.* (2000)
Plum	1 mM Sodium nitroprusside	Up to 120 days (Slower flesh reddening and lower levels of athocyanins)	Storage at 2 ºC with 85-90 per cent RH	Zhang *et al.* (2007)
Apple	DETANO dipping for 60s in a solution of 10 $mg1^{-1}$	170	Treatment solution preferably acidic pH 6.5.	Pristijono *et al.* (2008)

Flores *et al.* (2008) reported the ethylene production and respiratory rate of peach cv. Rojo Rito treated with NO were lower than those of control fruits. Treated fruits underwent a lesser loss of firmness during storage. A possible mechanism is

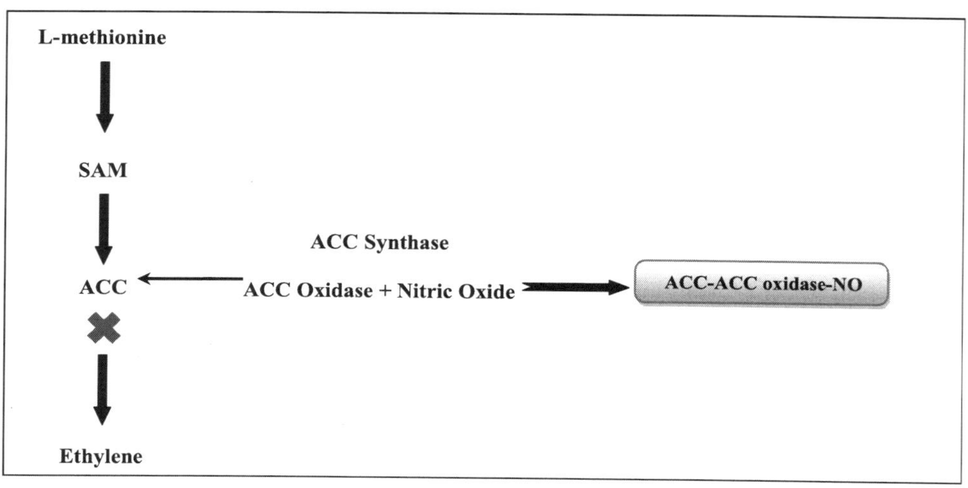

Figure 5: Mode of Action of Nitric Oxide.

Table 13: NO Associated Postharvest Biochemical Changes

Commodity	*Treatment Type*	*Biochemical Effects*	*References*
Strawberry	NO gas	Inhibition of ethylene production.	Leshem *et al.* (1998)
Bartlett Pears	NO gas	Yellowing was delayed 2 days.	Sozzi *et al.* (2003)
Peaches	NO gas	Inhibition of ACC oxidase, thus redirection of ethylene to MACC production and inhibition of lipoxygenase.	Zhu *et al.* (2006)
Strawberry	5 µmol 1^{-1} SNP aqueous solution	Inhibition of ethylene production, respiration rate, activitiy of ACC synthase and reduction of ACC content.	Zhu and Zhou (2007)
	SNP at 10 µmol 1^{-1}	Higher concentration harmed the fruits.	
	1 µmol 1^{-1} SNP	Its too low to significantly extend strawberry storage life.	
Longan	5 min dip in 1 mM sodium nitroprusside (SNP)	Modulation of the phenolic metabolism for reduced browning. Inhibition of the *in vitro* activities of PPO and POD.	Duan *et al.* (2007)
Plum fruit	SNP donor	Inhibition of pectin solubilisation and depolymerisation, reduced phenolic content, increase in titratable acidity, lower DPPH redical scavenging activity, chilling injury protection.	Zhang *et al.* (2007)
Apple slices	DETANO	Inhibition browning of fruits.	Pristijono *et al.* (2008)
Banana slices	SNP	Inhibition of ACO activitiy and transcription of gene MA-ACO1, PG, PME and endo-dippa-1, 4-glucanase and maintained higher contents of ASP and starch	Cheng *et al.* (2009)
Jujube fruit	NO fumigation	Inhibition of PPO and PAL activities, maintained a low total anthocyanin content and a high total phenol content and delayed the increase of soluble solids and decrease of vitamin C.	Zhu *et al.* (2009)

proposed that NO is bound to ACC oxidase to form an ACC oxidase-NO complex, leading to a decrease in ethylene production. The increase in concentration of ACC in NO-treated peaches may result in the redirection of ethylene to MACC production (Zhu *et al.*, 2006). Barman *et al.* (2004) found the similar result in mango chausa and also reported the nitric oxide reduce pericarp browning and reserve bioactive antioxidants in litchi. Zaharah *et al.* (2011) reported the mode of action of nitric oxide (NO) in inhibiting ethylene biosynthesis and fruit softening during ripening and cool storage of mango fruits. Hard mature green mango (*Mangifera indica* L. cv. 'Kensington Pride') fruits were fumigated with 20 uL L^{-1} No for 2 h at 21°C and allowed to ripen at 21 ± 1°C for 10 d, or stored at 13 ± 1 °C for 21 d. NO fumigation inhibited ethylene biosynthesis through inhibition of ACS and ACO activities leading to reduced ACC content in the fruit pulp which consequently, reduced the activities of fruit softening enzymes during ripening and cool storage.

Duan *et al.* (2007) investigated the effects of nitric oxide (NO) on enzymatic browning of harvested longan fruit in relation to phenolic metabolisms. Fruits were dipped for 5 min in 1 mM sodium nitroprusside (SNP), a nitric oxide donor, then packed in 0.03 mm thick polyethylene bags and finally stored for 6 days at 28°C. SNP treatment delayed pericarp browning, inhibited activities of PPO, POD and PAL and maintained a high total phenol content of longan fruit during storage. Furthermore, NO showed a significant inhibition of the *in vitro* activities of PPO and POD, indicating that the beneficial effect of NO was direct. Moreover, application of NO resulted in a lower pulp breakdown and maintained relatively high levels of total soluble solids and ascorbic acid.

Chapter 10

Controlled Atmosphere Storage (CA)

Introduction

Storage of fruits and vegetables an one of the ancient methods. CA storage is the advanced method followed by refrigeration. Commercial storage ammonia gas is used. With further advances in physiology and biochemistry it was found various gases are present in the fruits and vegetables O_2, CO_2, ethylene, nitrogen *etc.* in the tissues brought about revolution in storage of fruits and vegetables.

CA

Fruits and vegetablses are stored in controlled condition followed by refrigeration. It stand many break down process by maintaining an atmosphere of more CO_2 less than O_2 than normal air. As of today in advanced countries more than half of holding of apple and in Israll, citrus fruits are stand in CA storage. CA become a part of commercial storage of commodities. For individual commodities there are different atmosphere.

Technically CA implies addition or removal of gases resulting in an atmospheric composition substantially different from that of normal air. Thus CO_2, O_2, Co, ethylene, acetylene or nitrogen may be manipulated to attain various gas combinations. However, by common uses CA storage is the term used for increased CO_2, decreased O_2 and high nitrogen levels as compared with normal atmosphere.

Modified Atmosphere Storage

MAS means packaging in film bags and this also requires decrease in O_2 and an increase in CO_2 or nitrogen. The only difference between CA and MAS is that in MAS there is no effort to manipulated the concentration of various gases. The degree of controlled atmosphere of two is the degree of control of gases.

Gas Storage

is also used to distinguish it like CA and MA from the normal air storage. In gas storage atmosphere consists of one gas that is 100 per cent. For example the surrounding atmosphere that contains nitrogen only is known as nitrogen storage.

Partial Vaccum

Sub-atmospheric pressure and hypobaric storage, they all are synonymous terms. Hypobaric term is gaining popular usage. It is a type of controlled atmosphere storage with emphasis on reducing the pressure exerted on the storage material. This method not only reduces oxygen conc. but also increases the diffusion of ethylene by evacuation from the tissues of the fruits consequently extending the storage life of fruits (Wu and Solunkhe, 1972).

Metabolic Effects of CA

(1) Retarded Respiration

Respiration 3 types

a. Aerobic
b. Anacorbic
c. Combination of two end products

} Different and products are evolved

a. Aerobic respiration occurs when the O_2 supply is normal and results in the liberation of CO_2 and water.
b. CO_2 and ethyle alcohol
c. Rate of respiration is very high atmosphere gets saturated with CO_2, the rate of respiration is reduced. Practically respiration process continues even after that because the metabolic process of soft tissues are very complex. Neither high CO_2 nor low O_2 is the completely satisfactory method of changing whole chain of reaction envolved in respiration. This is evident by development or off flavour, soften or a complete break down of tissue before normal ripening process are control.

It was found out that the average rate of loss of carbohydrate in respiration was 1.2 and 1.4 times faster in normal air than in 10 per cent O_2 in nitrogen and between 1.35 and 1.55 times faster in the absence of CO_2 than in the presence of 10 per cent CO_2. Thus the fruits removed from conventially refrigerated storage exhibit the high rate of respiration than CA stored. It was also observed that CO_2 delays the onset of respiration rise in Avocado and reduce the rate of O_2 uptake at climacteric peak.

Acid Accumulation

It has been observed that some of organic acid and Amino acids are increased when the apple and pear *etc.* are stored in CA. Wankier (1970) and Wankier *et al.* (1970) when Apricots and Peaches were stored in CA. Storage, the CO_2 conclusion was higher than normal air at 34°F then there was an accumulation of succinic acid. This was accompanied by decrease of Malic and citric acid. Singh *et al.* (1970)

reported that when the Lambert Cherry fruits were stored in CA storage in which the conclusion of CO_2 was 10.5 per cent then the conclusion of tyrosine was reduced but the conclusion of μ amino butyric and maleric acid was increased. This comparision was made with the similar variety when stored by conventional refrigerator at 34°F.

Li (1963) all the canges that takes place in commodities under CA storage are not detrimental. Some of changes increase the quality instead example Anjou pear. When Anjou pear stored under CA storage, after 7 months they have 78 per cent more maleric acid than conventional methods. It was also found that CO_2 atmosphere seemed to check the normal decrease of acidity normally experienced in storage. They suggested the possible reasons for acid accumulation during CA storage might be (1) Lower respiratory activity (2) Increase CO_2 fixation (3) or the presence of less active enzyme that converts maleric acid to pyruvate or oxaloacetate (4) The presence of progressive increase of CO_2 in the CA storage atmosphere accomparised by a progressive decrease O_2 proved to be a important factor in chlorophyll degradation in beans at 45°F, in brocali apricot and peaches at 34°F and in asparign and lettuce cultivars great lakes at 50-51°F.

Acetaldehyde Formation

Browning occur because of acetyldehyde formation. When its formation is lower browning does not occurs. This is produced by faulty CO_2 and O_2 proportions in storage.

Increase in Sugars

In case of conventional store there is no change but in CA storage by using 2 per cent O_2 and 3 per cent CO_2 it was found out that Bantlet and Anjou pears the starch disappeared during the first week. Sugar showed no consistant differences except that sucrose appeared to decrease more rapidly in CA but not significantly. So CA stored fruits have more sugar after ripening.

Decrease in Alcohol Soluble and Protein

Total alcohol soluble nitrogen decreased at slower rate at CA stored fruits resulting in higher conclusion of alcohol soluble nitrogen at the end of the storage period. Protein nitrogen responded the same way *i.e.* it decreased at a slower rate in fruits stored in CA.

Pectin Changes

In case of Bartlett and Hardy pears when they were stored at 45°F and increase in soluble pectins was recorded but in case of yellow Newton apples the increase of soluble pectin was retarded by CO_2 storage. It was suggest that CO_2 has an effect on proton pectin hydrolysis. Soluble pectin content was much higher when higher temperature and no CO_2 were involved. Wankier (1970) reported that although the rate of pectin degradation is affected by time and condition of storage. CA stored apricot and peach fruit retain higher pectin than conventional methods.

Adverse effects of CA are many but major one are only two:- (1) Fultan (1907) reported the effect of CO_2 on storage. Reported when the fruits are stored at CO_2

saturated conditions fruits were damaged. Now it is confirmed the biochemical component of fruits change in unusual manner during CA storage. (2) This injury to reflected in 3 forms.

Injury of CO_2 in Storage

(1) Browning of the fleshy mesocarp.

(2) Tissue break down.

(3) Accumulation of certain organic acids.

Succenic Acid- 0.001M is toxic, Hulmie (1956) conducted an expt. With apple peel, he supplied succenate to respiting peel and found the respiration felt zero, with the result the tissue become brown and dead. In 1958 Smock$_1$ he also stated that if there is completely lack of O_2 in storage atmosphere and continues for several days fruits will suffocate and will become alcoholic and badly off flavour. Tissue Browning: takes place because of biochemical changes of tansins (are a complex assemblages of polyhydroxiphenol which offen habit no close structural relationship. The tannins can be distinguished with other phenol by their precipitating action of protein. However, this does not apply for chlorogenic and cafferic acid). In peaches 3 important tenins have been isolated. Dcatechines, Phlabatannins and Chlorogenic Acid. Intensity of browning is determined by percent of phenolic substances present in the fruit. The prunemesocarp which is near endocarp tissue was higher in enzymatic activity and that both phenolase and peroxydase enzymes are involved in tissue browning. Other studies also reports that phenolase and peroxidase active in apricot browning. Phenolase activity is correlated with the pH of fruit juice. At pH 2-2 the phenolase activitiy was zero, at pH 7 phenolase activity was maximum.

Controlled Atmosphere Storage, the Physiological and Practical Considerations: O_2, CO_2 Levels

(1) Devaux Effects

There are some changes in the pressure of gases inside and outside of commodities which takes place when the plant organs *i.e.* commoditieis are brought from one gas mixture to other. (Marellin, 1960 and Desaus *et al.*, 1962). It is influenced by the characteristics of the tissues, permeability of the cuticle Lenticels or stomata, volume of intercellular spaces and other anatomical features that change during ripening.

(2) The Physiological Effects of O_2 Concentration

(a) Repiratory rate and oxidation of substract are reduced. (b) Ripening is delayed and hence the life of the commodity is prolonged. (c) Chlorophyll break down is delayed. (d) C_2H_4 production low. (e) Rate of ascorbic acid losses is reduced. (f) Proportion of unsaturated fatty acid is changed. (g) Degradation rate of insoluble pectic compounds is not as rapid as in the normal air. All factors influenced by O_2 conclusion.

(3) Temperature - O_2 – C_2H_4 Inter Relationship

(a) C_2H_4 is not active as temperature close to freezing.

(b) On the hand at 70°F ethylene can not induce ripening if the O_2 level is very low about 1 per cent.

(c) Softening may be induced by C_2H_4 even if CO_2 and O_2 levels are neither too low nor too high.

(4) Physiological Effects of CO_2 Concentration

(a When the CO_2 level increases in the storage atmosphere, the quantity of CO_2 dessolved in the all are combined with some constituents also increases. This phenomenon is reversible and has been studied by Soudin 1972.

(b) High levels of CO_2 within the all generally head to the following physiological changes (1) Decrease in the synthetic reactions of ripening for example in case of proteins and pigments. (2) Inhibition of some enzyme activities for example succino-dehydrogenase, cytochromoxidase. (3) Decrease in production of volatiles. (4) Disturbed organic acid metabolism specially the accumulation of succinic acid. (5) Slackening in the break down of pectin substances. (6) Inhibiton of chlorophyll synthesis and fruit degreening particularly after early picking. (7) Alteration in the proportion of various sugars. For example in case of chestnut it has been observed that they were sweeten after they have stored in CA at low temperature and high CO_2.

(5) Combined Effect of O_2, CO_2 and Temperature

For the most of the fruit and vegetables optimum range of temperature 32-40°F, O_2 3 per cent and CO_2 0-5 per cent.

(6) Humidity and Ethylene during Storage

(a) Ethylene stimulate the ripening of green fruits. The degree of ripening induction of ethylene is a function of its conct. temperature, stage of fruit development, atmospheric composition.

(b) To obtained maximum retardation of ripening, ethylene should be removed from storage room or from the sealed package.

(c) Adding Pot. permagnate (Kmnou) is one of the most effective means of absorbing C_2H_4.

(d) In airtight controlled atmosphere storage room or packages, water can accumulate and condensed, fungi may develop even CO_2 is present in excers. To check this use of fungiside is recommended.

(7) Post-controlled Atmosphere Storage Behavior

(a) Removal of produce from cold atmosphere to air of ordinary temperature initiate a series aprupt changes:

(1) Firmness decreases markedly.

(2) Respiratory gas exchange increases.

(3) Tissue browning may appear particularly a long storage.

(4) The yellowing is some times slow and difficult.

(5) When controlled atmosphere conditions are well chosen the organoleptic properties of the fruit are frequently better than under common refrigerated storage (Ulrich, 1966).

(8) Long Ca Storage Treatments

(a) Injury may still occur even at recommended O_2 and CO_2 levels if the length of storage period is unduly prolonged. For example in apple and pear the storage life may be 40-60 per cent longer than in air and some times more according to temperature and variety (Marcellin, 1970).

(9) Short Ca Storage Treatments

(a) Fruits may withstand high CO_2 or very low O_2 conclusion for short time.

(b) High CO_2 conclusion in the storage atmosphere has an inhibitory effect on fungi development but can change the organoleptic quality of the fruit.

(c) Very low O_2 levels which are responsible for the fermentation for short period are being utilized during transport. The O_2 con. is 1 per cent.

(d) Use of liquid N_2 and eventually adding 1-2 per cent O_2 are gaining interest as a fruit treatment in Australia (Hall, 1968).

(e) Lipid N_2 is now being studied in the transport of grapes and peaches in Italy (Pratella and Tonini, 1970). The treatment of produce in N_2 even for a short period must be examined otherwise it may be injurious.

Chapter II

Chemical Changes during Ripening and Senescence

Introduction

During ripening fruits pass many physiological and biochemical process (catabolic and anabolic processes). These process are inversible processes and their processes can not be altered. Their rate can be checked by many methods. Colour change in range during ripening is the process of chlorophyll degradation and synthesis of carotenoid pigments. In case of tomatoes two process (Chlorophyll degradation and Lycopene synthesis). Softening of the fruits is another attribute. This is caused by break down of in soluble protopectin into soluble pectin or it may be due to hydrolysis of starch (sequence) or fats.

In some fruits and vegetables begin synthesis may also adversely affect the texture. Thayhencing of texture also takes place excellency. Flavour is also a characterstic feature which combined taste, smell and feel. Ripening, usually brings increase in simple sugars to given sweetness, decrease in organic acid and phenolics to minimize astringency and acidity and increase in volatile emanatious to give characteristics flavour of fruits.

Carbohydrates

Sugars of the fruits are because of hydrolysis of starch into sucrose, glucose and fruictose. The pleasing taste and flavour is because of a particular sugar to acid balance in fruits, attractive colour is also many times because of various blends of sugar and acids. Example by the anthocyanadin derivatie and whose the texture of fruit is due to structural poly succrides. In case of Alphonso mango during the process of ripening starch completely hydrolysed to form sucrose. Many workers who have studied the changes they all reported the gradual increase in glucose, fuictose and sucrose as the ripening process advances. Modi and Reddy (1967) reported 5 times increase in total pentose content and they observed the synthesis of fruictose was 1½ times more than of glucose. Most of the other soluble carbohydrate besides from starch they all are completely metabolise as fruits ripen. In case of Avocado they are completely hydrolise at full ripe stage. Structural carbohydrate decrease very slightly for example galacturonic acid did not change much even in over ripe stage of tomato.

Organic Acids

Non volatile organic acids are major cellular constituents which undergo changes during ripening of fruits. In case of mango 3 organic acids *i.e.* malic, citric and ascorbic acids have been detected. During the course of its development there is gradual sift from aicidity so less acidity. The pH at initial stage is 2.0 and at last 5.5. There is considerable decrease in pH as fruit ripe. The levels of citric, malic and ascorbic acid required to decrease by 10, 40 and 2.5 tones, respectively during ripening of mangoes. Malic acid was first to disappear followed by citric acid. This suggest possible catabolism of citvate bia malate. The pH of ripe mango is upto 6.3.

Amino Acids and Proteins

The importance of amino acid is very much because there are precursor of ethylene. Methionines, Balanine are the more important amino acid precursor of ethylene. A total of 69 amino acids are detected in mango. High turn over of amino acid and protein occur during ripening of mango fruits. At the climacteric of mango there is increase of glutamic acid, glutamine leucine and organine but at the onset of post clima... the levels of these amino acids decrease. In case of citrus and pear proline content incurred during ripening. In case of Avocado and Tomato there is not increase of protein content during the ripening.

Lipids

Low content of lipids in fruit and vegetables play an important role in texture, flavour and pigments *etc.* Triglycerides, diaglycerides, asterols, asterolestens, free fatty acids and hydrocarbons have been found as neutral lipids in tomatoes. Phospholipids of cytoplasm exert move import physiological than neutral lipids in reserved food materials Chloroplast in green tomatoes contains glycolipids and chlorophyll. Most important members of glycolipids are monogalactoryl, diglycerides and diagalactosyl diglycerides containing the higher unsaturated fatty acids in the diglyceride moiety. In case of ripening mango a considerable increase in total lipids and fatty acids have been observed. The main fatty acids present were palmatic, steanic, oleic, linoleic and linolenic unsaturated fatty acids increase more than saturated ones during mango ripening. In case of avocado poly unsaturated fatty acids stored at high O_2 levels increased, volatile fatty acids changes in ripening of bananas showed that free types increase rapidly and are responsible for flavour development of fruits.

Pigments

(1) Degradation of Chlorophyll

As the ripening proceeds green colour disappeares. This is due to an increase chloroplyllose activity in most of the cases. Chlorophyll content decrease in ripening fruits generally even though chlorophyll remains in ripening fruits example Pear, Tomato and Biochemical reaction of chlorophyll degradation is not fully clarified. In case of tomatoes no chlorophyllose activity was found even the chlorophyll degradation was at fast. Microscopic observations showed that the chloroplast disorganized much before the green colour disappear from the tissue. Changes in the conent of possible pigments in the tomato fruits with the degree of maturity (OD/100 gm fresh weight)

Table 14

Degree of Maturity	*Carotene*	*Lycopene*	*Xanthophyll*	*Chlorophyll*
Green	1.270	0	0.149	2.869
Greenish white	0.966	0	0.214	2.055
Greenish white with redishting	1.431	0.195	0.979	1.701
Ripe (dark red)	428,340.000	2,589,570.00	170,362.500	1.194

(2) Synthesis

It can be seen in tube that there is a drastic synthesis of caractenoid during the last steps ripening. A considerable increase in β carotene during ripening in Neelum, Totapari, Badami and Alphonso and Raspuri mangoes were reported by many workers. It was suggested that the change from green to yellow colour in citrus is marked by a loss of chlorophyll and appearing of carotenoid pigments and be used for carotenoid synthesis but this is not the case. In case of most of fruit and vegetable especially tomatos carotenoid synthesis takes place after the colour break. In case of Eureka lemon carotenoids decrease during ripening. While carotene synthesis is temporary independent, the lycopene synthesis is greatly affected by temperature optimum temperature of lycopene synthesis in tomato is between 60-70°F. It is inhibited at 85°F. The destruction occrs at less temperature.

Pectic Substances

These are mainly deposited between cell wall and middle lamella and act as cementing matereials. They are derivatives of polyagalacturonic acids and occurs in form of protopectin pectenic acid, pectin and pectic acid. Total pectic substances increase in amount during fruit development. While the content of soluble pectates and pectinates increase and total pectic substances decrease during the fruit ripening. This is the case with melon, Banana, citrus, strawberry and mango. As pectin changes fruit firmness decrease.

Volatile Products

The major chemical compounds found as esters of aliphatic alcohols and short chain fatty acids. These are found in noticeable amount when frit start ripening. In Banana the major volatile compound is isoamyle acetate, there is still uncertainity about the substance responsible for specific odour of most of the fruits. In some citrus fruit, Banana, Mango and Papaya some tenpenoil compounds could be responsible for specific odour. Treatment with ethylene which accelerates the normal metabolic process of maturation and ripening had a avourable effect on the aroma and more esters will be found specially ethyle acetate. The diurnal succession of day and night temperatures has a great influence on the volume and the composition of volatiles. Banana given a day temperature 85°F and 70°F in night produced 60 per cent more volatiles and their aroma was richer in esters than controls held at constant temperature of 85°F. Although it is known that alcohols and esters are formed when fermentation develops in the ripening fruit, the biochemical steps of aroma development are not yet known.

Enzyme

It is clear that many of the chemical and physical effects during ripening of fruits are attributed to enzyme action. For instance the softening of the fruits during ripening has been shown to be closely associated with increase in the pectinesterase and polygalacturorease activity in tomatoes as well as in avocados, pinapple, bananas and mangoes.

Catalase and Peroxidase

Rise in the activity of these enzymes associated with the high respiratory efficiency in mango varieties of mango encluding alphonso Neelum *etc.* Dilley (1972) suggested that catalase together with an appropriate oxidase may be involved in C_2H_4 production. Peroxidase may be relevant to the activities of senescing cells.

Glycolytic Enzymes

Those which are responsible for glycolytic break down of sugars. They are glucose phosphate isomerase, phosphor fructokinase, aldolose increase considerably during mango ripening.

Hydrolytic Enzymes

Accounts for hydrolysis of starch and weakening of cell wall. Amylase and cellulose are important hydrolytic enzymes. Whose activitiy increase in mango ripening. These enzymes do not bring about the softening of flesh. **Inventase**, it activity increases during ripening, along the increase activity of those enzymes which literate monosaccrides. **Transaminase:** These are aespansible for high turnover of aminoacial during mango ripening. **Citrate elevage enzyme:** With the increase activity of this enzyme during mango ripening suggests that citrate catabolism by this enzyme to acetyl CoA and orealoacetate may meet the heavy demand of these substances for synthetic processes.

NAD and NADP (Necotinamide adenine Dinucleotiale-NAD)

The conc. of these enzymes remain constant during ripening. The ratio of NAD PH/NAD and NADH/NAD increase considerably at the climacteric which indicates an active reductive metabolism during ripening. The changes in these ratios may be responsible for the regulation of certain enzymic pathways.

Enzymes of TCA Cycle and PPP

In most of the green fruits TCA cycle is the main pathway in the aspiration of green and yellow banana and the activity of pyrubeate decarboscylous, seems to increase in the cause of ripening. During the early ripening stages enzymes of PPP are active indicating that the substrate for protein synthesis are being fabricated.

Chlorophyllase

Activity increases as the chlorophyll degradation takes place as in banana but it may not be relevant to ripening. In case of tomato also there was no chlorophyllase activitiy during the ripening processes. Chlorophyll break down may proceed during cold storage without marked changes in other ripening attributes. The other enzymes which increase in ripening are fatty acid synthatase is closely associated in case of Avocado which is dependant on protein synthesis.

Enzyme Inhibitors of Unripe Fruits

Spencer (1965) suggested that the changes in the metabolic pathways, the activities of individual enzymes and the rate limiting reactions could be due to many causes including synthesis and destruction of enzymes, substract and cofactor, condition of pH and temperature and presence of inhibitor. The presence of heat labile and non dialigible enzyme inhibitors has been deducted in unripe fruits of mango, Banana and papaya which inhibits the activity of catalase, perosidase and amylase. The inhibitors have been shown to protein like which are stable at cold and freezing temperature. These inhibitors disappear during ripening and may regulate the oxidative metabolism of fruits. In the case of unripe mangoes the inhibitors of similar type have observed for various other enzymes like inventase, cellulose, glucose-6 phosphate, phosphofruktokinase, acid phosphatase and glutanic dehydrogenase. All of which increase during ripening. The fruit enzymes pectin esterase aldolase, glucose-6 phosphate dehydrogenase, 6-phospho gluconic acid dehydrogenase, malic enzyme and liver catalase were not inhibited by unripe fruit inhibitors.

Regulation of Enzyme Activity by β-carotene and Fatty Acids

The subject of regulation of enzyme activity in an area when intermediate any metabolism, Enzymology and molecular mechanisms meet. Now, there are 3 types of enzymes. (1) A class of enzymes that are inhibited by unripe mango inhibitors but not by fatty acids or β carotene. (2) A class of enzymes that are not inhibited by unripe mango inhibitors but are inhibited by fatty acid and β carotene. (3) A class of enzymes that are activated by fatty acids and/or β carotene but there are in numerable missing links yet to be found. Some opf the links which are missing as photochrome and absessive acid and influence of other auxins and Gibbherellins. Many other forms of control exhist in cellular system such as differences in the half life of an enzyme, Permeability factors and access of the enzyme to its substract in vivo which should be taken considerate on while examining fruit tissue.

Chapter 12

Regulation of Ripening and Senescence

Postharvest Treatments

Chemical Modification

Use of growth regulators other than mineral nutrition:

1. Chemicals that delay the ripening and senescence.
2. Chemicals which hasten ripening and senescence.
3. Chemical that may delay or hasten the ripening and senescence.
4. Auxin- ethylene interrelations on ripening.

1. Chemicals that Delay Senescence and Ripening – 7 Points

a) Kinins and kinetins.

b) Gibberellins.

c) Some auxins (C/PA and NoA).

d) **Growth retardants**

   (1) MH

   (2) Alar (B_9)

   (3) CCC

   (4) C/Pc

   (5) IPC

   (6) MeNA

e) **Metabolic inhibitors**

   (1) Cycloheximide

(2) Actinomycin-D
(3) Vitamin K
(4) Malic Acid
(5) Ethylene oxide
(6) Na DHA

f) **Ethylene absorbents**

g) **Some fumigants**
(1) Methyle formate
(2) Methylebromide
(3) Benolate

2. Chemicals that hasten Ripening and Senescence

a) Ethylene and ethylene releasing compounds.
(1) Ethephon (ethrel)
(2) CPTA (2-4-chlorophenoyl thio-triethyl amino hydro-chloride
(3) NIA series compounds

b) Absciasin

c) Ascorbic acid and β hydroxi ethylene hydrazine (BoH)

d) Aceteline and calcium carbide

e) Alcohals
(1) Ethenol
(2) Hexanol and others

3. Chemicals that may hasten as well Delay the Process of Ripening and Senescence

2, 4-D; 2, 4, 5-T; 2, 4, 5-TP; IAA; NAA

1. Chemical that Delay Ripening

TBZ (Thiabendazole)

Kinin and Kinetin

In general, the cytokinin, BA and kinetin shown to delay the chlorophyll degradation and senescence of vegetables like spinach, Brocoli *etc.* The retardation of yellowing by maintaining high protein level by applied tissue. This inference become and significant under prolonged storage or higher temperatures. After the crop is harvested the general degradation sets in this results in destruction of soluble RNA. Thus protein synthesis slows ddown and the mechanism of protein formation disturbed, the pigments and other constituent disintegrate. Salunkhe and Coworners (1962) explained the primary step in the degradation of the soluble RNA involves the loss of end group adenine. If at this stage BA is applied this supplement the adenine group and restored the soluble RNA molecule. The protein synthesis is maintained and treated stuff should be maintained for longer time. In commercial practice the cytokinins are sometime combined with other growth regulators to instance the senescence. When BA were combined with 2, 4-D and sprayed on yellowing cauliflower, the senescence was significantly delayed.

Gibberellins

The postharvest treatment of GA markedly retard the ripening of Guava, Banana *etc.* This was due to retarded respiratory rate, retarded climacteric and delayed colour change. In pears because of GA treated, pears could not prevented from ripening because of inadequate permeability. In case of citrus, the effects of GA application are retarded chlorophyll disappearance, increased peel firmness, delayed accumulation of carotenoids on navel oranges and higher TSS and ascorbic acid in Lisbon lemons but on the contrary GA has no effect on fruit quality on valeneia oranges and grapefruit.

Some Auxins (CIPA and NoA)

Preharvest foliar applications of NoA at 25 ppm or CIPA at 25 ppm delayed the physicochemical deterioration of coorg mandarins in storage. The improved marketable condition of treated fruit after storage was due to reduced weight loss and retention of vitamin C.

Growth Retardants

MH chicks the storage sprouting of onion, radish, carrot, turnip, sugar beets and potatoes. The effects of MH on ripening process varied with different types of fruits and may depend on the application time and amount of chemical obsorbed. If the mangoes are treated with hot water 10°C for 10 minutes, storage life is increased. If the mangoes are dipped in 1000-2000 ppm solution, the effects on storage life was further increased. Similar effects were obtained in case of tomatoes. In case of Sapota, it hastens the ripening and increased the respiration rate and induced high transpiration rate.

Alar (NN′ dimethyl amino succinamic acid). Increased fruit firmness, better fruit colour and early maturation are some of the effects are Alar when applied before maturation. Alar has no effect on ripening as the postharvest treatment. However, this was found to be effective in increasing the longevity of some of vegetable and Musroom. It presences the chlorophyll in leaves of beans and some other plants. Alar and ethrel were significantly effective in inhibiting the synthesis of solanin in potatoes under storage.

CCC

This was effective in retarding senescence in some of vegetables, self life of leaf lettuce was doubled.

CIPC, IPC, MeNA

Vaporized CIPC has given excellent sprout control in potatoes upto a year in 10°C storage at a dose of 1 gram per 1.25 kilograms. MeNA was less effective, the quantity required to obtained same results were 1 gram/1.81 kilograms. Foliar sprays of IPC reduce the rate of respiration, ripening and spoilage of sapota fruits during storage Ascorbic Acid was retained, although there was slight reduction in the total sugar content of apota fruits treated with 100 ppm IPC.

Metabolic Inhibitors

Cycloheximide and Actinomycin D

Flesh softening, chlorophyll degradation and ethylene synthesis were severely inhibited by cycloheximide treatments. As a result of application (Cycles...) the ripening process proceeded very slow. Similar was the case with actinomycin-D. Actinomycin D is more strong, if applied on the fruits and then ethylene is applied, then ethylene will not be as effective.

Vitamin K

K_1, K_3 and K_5, vitamin K_5 whose active conc. ranges from.05 to.005 per cent prolongs the shelf life and adds nutritive value to a variety of foods. Vitamin K can be considered as preservative with many merits in fruit juice. It has germicidal properties.

Malic Acid

Malic acid in amyl-acetate retarded the ripening of Jamaica Bananas, pinapple, citrus and other disiduous fruits.

Ethylene Oxide

May be an endogenous metabolic and antagonist of ethylene. Higher conc. of ethylene oxide or longer times of exposure prevented ripening in many fruits including mango and tomato.

NaDHA

This inhibits the respiratory enzyme activity. 0.5 per cent treatment with Na DHA delayed the ripening and reduced the rate of respiration of strawberry fruits.

CO (Carbon Monoxide)

It is found to be effective in prolonging the life of Mushrooms.

Ethylene Absorbants

Waxing, low O_2, high CO_2 and some time ripening inhibitors are combined to prolong the storage life. Hypoparic storage is such where these inhibitors are used.

(1) Braminated activated carbon

(2) Molecular sieve – 5A

(3) Celite with KMn O_4 (PURAFIL)

Some Fumigant

Methyl Bromide and Methyl formate. In case of mango when Methyle Formate was used then, besides from delaying mango fruits it gave maximum inhibition of ripening through out storage temperature of 20 days at ambient temperature. Methyle Bromide is less effective in case of mango.

2. Chemicals that Hasten Ripening and Senescence

(1) Ethylene and Ethylene releasing components Ethepion, CPTA *etc.*

(2) Abscisin: Accelerate senescence in detalhed fruits and leaves./Abscissoc Acid treatement of oranges resulted in accelerated breakdown of chlorophyll and increased synthesis of carotenoid.

(3) Ascorbic acid and β ethyle hydrazine: Ascorbic acid and CUEDTA and BOH were found to induce ethylene formation when sprayed before harvest. But when these chemicals were provide postharvest dip no chemical provide similar degreening rate.

Acetylene and Calcium Carbide

Degreening can be restored by burning leaves stems *etc.* These release ethylene. Communically calcium carbide treatment is given to accelerate acetylene. Ethylene is 100 times more effective than acetylene especially in case of Bananas.

Alcohals

In case of persimmon fruits ripening response was obtained as a result of ethanol addition. Boe (1966) found that ethylene injections caused differential ripening of tomato fruits. Several forms of alcohol is used for tomatoes, Hexanol is more effective.

Fatty Acids

In case of figs, it is ancient practice to apply oil. Studies conducted on various types of oil and it was found that vegetable oils were most effective. Mineral oils were inferior most oil treatment induces respiration and ethylene production.

3. Chemicals that may Hasten and Delayed Ripening and Senescence

2, 4-D, 2, 4, 5-T, 2, 4, 5-TP

In case of citrus storage life was prolonged by application of 2, 4-D and 2, 4, 5-T mainly as a result of delayed degreening. Storage quality of 2, 4, 5-T treated fruits were also improved, there was less physiological loss in weight, highly marketable per cent and less vitamin C loss in otourd coorg mandarin oranges. All these treatments were given postharvest. When preharvest treatment were given (2, 4-D and 2, 4, 5-T @ 100 ppm and 2, 4, 5-TP @ 25 ppm) ripening was hastened in Sapota fruits. It has been reported that 2, 4, 5-T accelerate the ripening of Fig fruits indirectly by the production of ethylene. The time of auxin application has the pronounced effect or response. Auxin stimulate the synthesis of ethylene of tomato fruits, depends upon the maturity at the time of treatments. Treated immemature tomato fruits produce more ethylene than those treated at the pink stage. This is why the treatment of 2, 4-D has little effect on the respiration of mature green tomatoes.

IAA and NAA

NAA is used more extensively than IAA because it is cheaper and easily available, its action does not differ much. It has been shown that IAA and NAA inhibit the activity polygalacturonase in the early stages of tomato ripening but later and hence delayed ripening. Similar delaying effect on ripening on some variety of pineapple and Basrai banana was observed as a result of NAA application. In case of onion bulbs, the storage life is also prolonged when 0.4 ppm NAA is used as foliar spray. In case of application and pears the results are variable. Preharvest sprays of NAA were reported to accelerate ripening and shorten storage life but many other workers did not find either increase ripening rate or deterioration of storage quality on the fruits stored with NAA. NAA accelerate ripening incertain summer varieties an apple and pears but not on late ripening varieties.

Auxin-Ethylene Interrelation on Ripening

It has been demonstrated that some interaction occur between auxins and Ethylene. When 2, 4-D was applied prior to treatment with ethylene, the accelerated effect of ethylene on ripening was reduced, however no such inhibition of ripening was obtained if ethylene was applied first. Hormonal action is doubtful here because one was applied after the other, effective interrelation is applied with joint application. In general the effect of auxin on ripening is retardation rather acceleration. Ripening was hasten mostly in cases when auxin conc. use were high resulting metabolic damage.

Possible Mechanism of Chilling Injury

The fundamental mechanism associated with chilling injury is tentatively as follows:

A progressive devine the capacity of fruit for oxidative phosphorelations occur with exposure to low temperature. This could lead to shortage of high energy typically ATP needed for maintenance for cell organization in the presence of enzymatic process constantly tending to disrupt the system. Because of the resultant shortage energy a net break down of complex cellular organs followed. The attendant loss of tissue organization as result of chilling could explain the observe increase in cell membrane permeability, susceptibility to decay, accumulation of metabolite and increase in oxygen increase. Associated with ATP shortage rind pitting could result from an accumulation of toxic volatiles under the cuticle which were released across the permeable membranes. These volatiles including acetaldehyde may originate from sub-oxidation of substrates as a consequence of low energy supply.

Packaging House Operations

The produce is subjected to various treatments before it sent to storage or markets. These things are common practice in advanced countries and the backward countries do not adopt these practices. In these countries only the produce is processed to the extent that they are for markets.

Shorting, grading, degreening, bunching, chemical treatment and precooling *etc.* adopted. This differs with various crops. These packing house operations are essential for distant markets. These are as follows:

1. Curing
2. Degreening (Polyethylene filters are used) – Physiology
3. Precooling:
   (1) Air colling
   (2) Hydrocooling
   (3) Vacuum cooling Half-cooling time
4. Washing
5. Drying
6. Waxing
7. Grading
8. Sizing
9. Disinfestation treatments
10. Colour adding

Curing

The product is allowed to recover such harvesting injury usually at the normal temperature in air, usually the crops are potato, onion, garlic *etc.* This process is also termed as healing process. The changes that occur includes reduction of moisture in onions for same time. This helps in storage. This is done in ambient temperature. In potato they are held at 10.33°C for two days then 4.44-7.22°C at 10 days at 90 and 95 per cent R.H.

Degreening

Means the removal of green colour and its replacement of that colour as appeals by consumer. Generally done by applying ethylene or similar metabolic controller. This is done usually in case Banana, Mango, papaya, citrus and tomatoes. The length of time of degreening is depends upon degree of maturity at which it is harvested. This process is done in case of papaya by carbide treatment for 12-24 hours. This is done in specially treatment room at controlled temperature and RH 1: 50,000 is applied. The best temperature 26.65°C and RH is 85-92 per cent RH. For degreening polyethylene films are used. Small contractors used baskets, Jar *etc.* 0.2 mm thickness of polyethylene film is used. Depending upon the nature of fruit and degree of maturity and the colour, the operation takes about 3 days time. The physiology of degreening is that when ethylene is applied it accelerate the without affecting the synthesis of carotenoid pigments.

Precooling

Before keeping the fruits in storage, the precooling is done, so that tissues may not injure.

Preconditioning

This is the operation where fruit or vegetable are kept in higher temperature. Aircooling is done by circulating cool air, but the temperature should not be below 30°F depending of nature of fruit.

Hydrocooling

Water is used for cooling purpose. This is used in leafy vegetable to retain the texture and freshness. This method has on disadvantage, when water is allowed to come to contact, the susceptibility of fruit to decay increased, The citrus fruits which are precooled by this method, the fruits are treated with fungicides which should be tolerable limits.

Vacuum Cooling

Best and rapid method of precooling for leafy vegetable. The principle applied is that of evaporating cooling. In case of head lettuce vacuum cooling takes place with 3-4 minutes with dropping temperature 80°F to 32°F and this case there is no injury.

Half Cooling Time

This term indicates the time required to reduce the initial temperature difference between the fruit and cooling medium by one half.

- ☆ Suppose half cooling time is 12 hours.
- ☆ Initial temperature 26.66°C
- ☆ Suppose cool water 4.44°C
- ☆ The initial temperature 4.44°C difference
- ☆ The half difference will be 15.55°C.
- ☆ To come down the temperature from 26.66°C to 15.55°C takle 12 hrs.

Washing

If the hydrocooling is done washing is completed if it is not done, the washing is necessary and this should be at ambient temperature. The water may be hard or soft soap and any detergent material may be used. In case when the water is soft the common detergent is used as sodium metasilicate. When it is hard trisodium phosphate is used. Some fruits like strawberry washing operation is not done, if done no detergent is used. Musk melons, cucumber and sweet potato are brushed and whipping dry and not directly washed. Some time cleaner are used. The most common is Dowicide A. hexamine.

Drying

Removal of excess surface water from the fruit or vegetable. This done by blowing not air on fruit or vegetables.

Waxing

Most of fruits and vegetables have waxy surface while washing this coveing is removed pently or completely. Because of this, the looses natural appearance.

Therefore, a fine coating of some natural waxes is done so the fruits and vegetables retain its original colour. By providing this coating, necessary protection against the decay organism is done. Under refrigerator storage this is not as important as non refrigerated storage. Several wax formulations have been developed. Synthetic or natural rasies are added to more shine or glass to the commodity which is treated. The suitly emulsifier are mixed. They are of two types of wax coat (1) Water wax emulsions, (2) Solvent type waxes.

Water wax emulsions are safer to use, solvent type waxes are highly feameable. The first type is used without necessity of drying of fruit prior to waxing. For solvent type waxes the surface must be free from moisture to get shine. Sugar cane wax, carnauba wax, Thermoplastic terpene resin, shellac resin *etc.* are the common types which are used for the preparation of coating materials. Trietharnolamine and olic acid generally used as emulsifier. Some time some fungicids are also added to this. Waxes may be applied by brushing, foaming or dipping but different methods should be adopted. Poaming is a satisfactory means of application. Water waxes are sprayed from hydrolic or numatic nozels. Dipping involves placing the fruit or vegetable in a dip tank for wax emulsion for 30 seconds.

Grading

is subject which is very well concerned in various countries and within country. Various methods are used for domestic purposes. Different grades are based on soundness, firmness, cleaniness, size, weight colour, shapes maturity and freedom from foreign matter and diseases, insect damage or mechanical injury. For foreign trades the standards have been defined by (1) ECE (Economic commission for Europe, Geneva, 1954), (2) OECD (Organization for economic cooperation and development, 1970). 3 general categories of a protocol classification could be:

(A) Extra, class is the best class

(B) I class

(C) Second class

Grading may be done manual or mechanical.

Sizing

After grading the fruits are sized for uniformity, sizing is done is useful small scale packaging. For large purposes various sizing devices are used based on either shape and weight of the produce. Hydrohandling is a method being developed for shorting fruits and the system utilizing both shape and weight of fruit in sizing.

Desinfestation Treatment

Fruit places are most important pest in horticultural crops. Papaya, Mango, Melons *etc.* are highly susceptible fro fruit fly attack. For various commodities there are different methods. For papayas. 3 methods are used.

(1) Vapour heat treatment.

(2) EDB fumigation treatment (Ethylene dibromide).

(3) Irradiation.

In varpour heat treatments the papays are tagged in open field lugs are first preconditioned by waxing at 43.33°C for 11 hours under a RH of about 40 per cent. After preconditioning, fruits are exposed to 100 per cent RH for 8.75 hours at 43.33°C fruit temperature. After treatment papayas are cooled to about atmospheric temperature with circulating air and then packed.

In EDB treatments packed papayas are emerged in hot water at 48.80°C for 20 minutes then cooled in sunny water for 20 minutes. Then they are treated with EDB with dosage of 0.3268 kg per 30000 cm^3 for few hours at fruit temperature not lower than 21.11°C.

Irradiation, Gamma irradiate is used as a dose of 21 krad. The fruit can tolerate upto 100 krad.

Colour Adding

Applicable on those fruits where suitable dyes are available to give attractive natural colour. In citrus after degreening colour is pale. In this case colouring is done by citrus Red No. 2 (1-(2, 5 dimethorey phenylazo) – 2 naphthal, @ 2 ppm. Some times these colours are added to waxes before waxing of fruits. These dyes which are added to waxes require one treatment. Colour waxes are used in colour varieties of potatoes, sweet potatoes carrot *etc.* They unhanced colour as the vegetable is freshly ripe.

Packaging

Means fruits and vegetable are wrapped in small packaging for consumers or for bigger parties. They may be of different types as the case may be. When any kind of packaging is used then it provide some short of modified atmosphere storage. This packaging preserves the quality, therefore best material must be used.

Benefits of Packaing

There are 6 advantages of good packaging.

(1) Serves as an efficient handling unit.

(2) Serves as convenient wareshouse or home storage units.

(3) Protects quality and reduces waste may be 5 type.

   (a) Protection from mechanical damage.

   (b) Protection against moisture loss.

   (c) It may provide beneficial modified storage.

   (d) Provides clean or sanitary products.

   (e) Prvent from pilferage.

(4) Provides service and sales motivation.

(5) Reduces cost of transport and marketing.

(6) Facilitates use of new modes of transportation.

Type of Containers and Packaging Materials

(1) **Harvesting or field containers:** Applicable in case of fruits.

(2) **Containers in the shed or packing house:** Will be different depending upon the commodities. They are used in shed or packing house.

(3) **Shipping containers:** are used for transporting. They should be reasonably desirable size, having tags containg variety, grade *etc.* Wooden containers have been used with success apart of wooden containers there are fibre board cartons, Paper board cartons, there are Bulk boxes or pallet bins. These are compreatively larger in size and require repacking in smaller size containers. There is lot of necessity of packing in tropics and subtropics which is unfortunately neglected.

(4) **Consumer packaging with plastics:** Fruits are temporarly packed in leaves baskets. Suitable for date palm, papaya, citrus *etc.* These baskets are also made of bamboo. Flexible plastics are used now a days for packaging. These are of 4 main types.

  (a) **Polyethylene films (low density):** For greens like lettuce *etc.* cast polypropylene films is used.

  (b) **Cellopane (is the regenerated cellulose):** There are various types and various colours.

  (c) **Rubber hydrochloride (also known as pliofilm)**

  (d) **Polyvinyl chloride film (PVC):** They are of various types. The most common is cellulose acetate if there is necessity, then these films are punched and make perforated so that ventilation is possible.

Chapter 13

Postharvest Handling of Mango Fruits

Mango (*Mangifera indica* L.) has assigned the status of 'King of fruits' in the world due to its great importance in cultural, socio-economic and religious significance since the age old. Owing to its origin in Indo-Myanmar region possessing the delicious fruit quality with richness in vitamins and minerals. The genus *Mangifera* L. is monotypica. The genus *Mangifera* of the order Sapindales and family Anacardiaceae are restricted to the tropical Asia. The highest concentration of species found in the western part of Myanmar-Siam-Indochina. Mango is important fruit crop in India covered largest area 34.9 per cent of total fruit area and second highest in production 20.9 per cent of total fruit production of country, ranging its cultivation from the near costal areas to the Shivalik foot hills. Enormous utility of mango in various forms and kinds have attracted the attention of tropical and subtropical world for understanding its nature of growth, flowering and fruiting and their physiological manipulation to the benefits of growers and consumers. The mango industry in India has not expanded to the extent it should primarily because of lack of proper coordination and integration of postharvest management. This is in spite of the fact that fresh mango export of country in 41279.97 MT of value 28542.85 Lakh and mango pulp 174860.33 MT value 77294.76 Lakhs. Till recently research efforts in various aspects of postharvest handling were taken up by various workers and Institutes in their individual capacity according to national or local needs. The development of processable cultivars and technologies for promotion of processing and value addition need to be upgraded for the diversification of mango products.

Maturity and Harvesting Indices

Traditionally mango is harvested based on judgements by the growers by observing the appearance of the fruit. The selection of suitable maturity indices for harvest is very important. The quality and the postharvest life of mango fruit depend on the maturity stage at harvest. Therefore, the fruit has to be harvested at the suitable stage of maturity in order to develop the optimum sensory quality attributes and extended postharvest life. Immature fruits are more sensitive to chilling injury during cold storage and may fail to ripen adequately. Fruit harvested at over mature stage is highly susceptible to mechanical damage such as bruising, decay and water loss, resulting in quality. Over matured fruit show defects like jelly seeds or jelly pulp after harvest. Therefore, suitable maturity indices for harvesting are very important in order to minimize the quantitative and qualitative losses. Generally, physical, physiological and chemical parameters are used to define the maturity stage. Physical methods to determine maturity in mango include softness of the cheek, peel colour, development of shoulder and specific gravity. These factors are very useful, but their application depends on the type of mango, region of cultivation and type of market and consumers. Age of the fruit is also considered as a simple method to confirm maturity, calculated from induction, full bloom and fruit set. Generally, harvest maturity in mango is reached about 12 to 16 weeks after fruit set. However, days from full bloom is most recommended, because they can be implemented as a standardized factor. The age of fruit (days) at a certain harvest maturity based on full bloom or fruit set varies according to different geographical regions and cultivation conditions.

Mangoes for shipping to distant markets or for long-term storage are harvest at the mature-green stage while still firm and the ripening will continue after harvest. Furthermore, maturity level at harvest is a crucial factor for the development of acceptable flavour quality during ripening. In addition, mango fruit accumulates dry mature during fruit development and becomes denser as it matures. Therefore, specific gravity was considered as a possible maturity index. Specific gravity generally ranges from 0.97 to 1.04, but sometimes it does not contribute to determining fruit maturity. During fruit maturation, soluble solids content (SSC) tends to increase while titratable acidity (TA) decreases. Tharanthan *et al.* (2006) titratable acidity increased from the sixth to the tenth weeks after fruit set and then with increase in fruit maturity a decline in titratable acidity was noted. Soluble solid content is not generally used as a commercial maturity index for mangoes but it complements other indices such as shoulder formation and flesh colour and for most markets mangoes have to be harvested at about 9-10 per cent soluble solid contents. Some mango cultivars are characterized by a strong taste and the SSC and TA or the SSC/TA can contribute to determining the suitable maturity stage for harvest. Sugars acids and phenolic compounds are the primary taste components in the fruit. SSC/TA ration commonly indicates ripeness and taste for some markets; the higher the ratio the sweeter the fruits. Flavour (taste and aroma) is an important quality trait that determines to a great extent, the consumer acceptance of the fruits. Flavour is tase plus odour and is mainly composed of sweetness, sourness and aroma that correspond to sugars, acid and volatile compounds. Flavour is determined primarily by genetic factors and it can be affected due to preharvest conditions, postharvest handling, packaging operations and storage.

Changes in mango aroma can be attributed to transformational changes in fatty acid profile (from palmitic to palmitoleic acids) during ripening and fruit can reach their best flavour if harvested after the start of ripening. Increase of glycosidically-bound aroma compounds (terpenes) were observed in the flesh of Kensington Pride mangoes as maturity progressed. Optimum skin colour is an important fruit quality parameter that affects consumer acceptance and preference. The obvious noticeable change during ripening is skin colour change from dark green to olive green or reddish or orangish yellow or yellow that forms a base colour. Some cultivars show reddish bluish skin colour mainly due to the presence of anthocyanins. Skin colour changes are due to the disappearance to chlorophyll and the appearance of other pigments (carotenoids and/or anthocyanins). Carotenoids are the predominant pigments in yellow cultivars. Presence of the anthocyanin phenondin-3-galacytosa has been reported in the skin of some types of cultivars. However, skin colour is not considered as an adequate maturity index because it is commonly observed after the fruit has started to soften, in addition to that skin colour is usually not very uniform in several mango cultivars. Uniform colour development is observed in yellow cultivars, but some cultivars do not change the green skin colour much. Skin colour development is greatly influenced by the fruit position on the tree and fertilizer application practices, among other factors. Flesh colour changes are uniform when fruit advances in maturity stages and, therefore, it can serve as adequate maturity index. Although, it is a destructive index, it is used as a maturity index in several producing regions, because it is consistent. Carotenoids are responsible for the attractive flesh colour and at advanced maturity, the flesh is usually yellow to orange. Although, it is difficult to establish standard maturity indices for mangoes due to the diversity of cultivars and growing conditions, it is essential to establish them for a particular cultivar, growing region and for local or export markets. The development of a non-destructive flesh colour sensor for mango would help the harvesting team to correlate physical indices such as shape and size with flesh colour in order to determine the appropriate maturity stage at harvest.

Harvesting

Harvesting fruit before or after the ideal picking date and any harvesting methods that cause mechanical damages such as bruising or cuts on the fruit surface will affect fruit quality. The cut or bruised fruits are easily infected with decay causing fungi such as *Aspergillus* sp. and *Botryodiplodia, Diplodia natalensis.* Mechanical injury at harvest can cause 'spongy tissue', where, the symptom is expressed as desiccated spongy like tissue in ripe fruits and the symptom can be observed only when the fruit is cut open. At this specific spongy region, the flesh remains unripe due to biochemical disturbances and deposition of non hydrolysed starch taking place during storage. The affected part of the flesh was reported to show low pH, sugar, ascorbic acid content and β-carotene content and altered amylase and invertase activitiy. Mango is harvested manually, usually with the help of some harvesting aids and multiple harvesting is adopted since all the fruits are not matured at the same time. Fruits are harvested from tall trees by using poles fitted with bags adapted with a scissors or knife. Ladders are used in some regions and hydraulic lifts are not common. It is to harvest fruits when the temperature is not high, which will reduce field heat in the fruit and thus would maintain it for longer periods by reducing metabolic activity. However, cultivars with high sap or latex content should not be harvested very early in the day due to high latex flow early mornings. Fruits are normally picked from the lower side of the tree in order to avoid sap oozing on the fruit below. The stem will snap easily with a slight pull for the mature green fruit that is ready for picking, although, the use of scissors is recommended when possible. Sap injury or burn of the skin affects fruit quality by affecting the skin colour and promoting decay development and also affects the skin of the pickers. Mango sap and its negative effects can be reduced by adopting different methods such as by using detergent dips and sprays prior to de-stemming under water using lime, picking without stems onto a harvesting aid such as racks and dipping or spraying detergent on the fruit immediately, cleaning latex from fruit skin, washing the fruit after harvesting and use of harvesting rack was recommended as the most effective method which reduces sap burn down to about 16 per cent.

The harvested fruits are kept in cool place away from direct sunlight and heat to prevent acceleration of the metabolic activities for enhancing the shelf life. Fruits are segregated for immature, undersized, damaged, bruised, scarred and ripe fruits and placed in clean disinfected shallow plastic crates, bags, sacks and baskets are to be avoided as these generally result in mechanical damage and bruising. Fruits should never be placed on the bare soil to avoid the infection by pathogens. The components of the postharvest management of mango are grading, handling, packaging, pre-cooling, cold storage, transportation and processing and value addition. Appropriate management of temperature and humidity at each stage of handling is vital to maintain high fruit quality. The proper temperature management minimizes respiration and other physiological activities and microbial infection. Fungicide treatment helps in preventing anthracnose disease which causes fruit rot and maintains the quality of fruits at a high level. Besides, maintaining high quality, the fruits are presented to the consumers in attractive and acceptable condition by washing to remove dirt, residues and stains of latex and waxing to brighten the appearance.

Handling

Mango is one of the main export earners among fruits. Alphonso cultivar of mango is being exported from India in a large quantities. This cultivar, however, suffers from the problem of spongy tissue. Minimizing the postharvest losses have been the main challenge. Some of the methods used for extending the shelf life of mango are low temperature storage and other technologies, which are as follows:

Shelf-life

Various approaches such as low temperature, controlled atmosphere (CA, modified calcium and anti-ethylene compounds and plant growth regulators have been tested to extend storage life of mango fruit with acceptable quality. Chemical treatments for delaying ripening and irrigation extend shelf-life of fruit on tree and proper packaging and shrink wrapping extend the shelf-life in storage. A temperature range from 5 to 15°C for the storage of different cultivars of mango. The ideal temperature range for long shelf-life has, however, been found to be 12-15°C. Mangoes are highly prone to low temperature injuries, which manifest in the form of the loss of flavour and development of undesirable softening. Keeping mangoes in polythene bags with 0.5 per cent ventilation is, therefore, suggested for storing them at low temperature. The shelf-life of mango fruits is only 5 to 6 days under ambient conditions, which can be increased efficiently, if the rates of biological activities and/or changes are reduced by pre and/or postharvest treatments. The preharvest treatment of SA (200 ppm) one week prior to the harvesting in cv. Amrapali was found effective in delaying the ripening cum senescence processes through suppression of ethylene production rate (0.20 µl C_2H_4/kg/h) and helped in maintaining the postharvest quality through better retention of soluble solid concentrates (SSC) (27.72°B), titratable acidity (0.53 per cent), ascorbic acid (32.52 mg/100 g) and total antioxidant content (11.85 µmol Trolox/g Fresh Weight). The Sa treatment was also found to effectively influence the pectin methylesterase activitiy (0.167 µmol acid/min) as well as the lipid peroxidation (2.26 µmol/g Fresh weight) during storage in order to extend the fruit shelf-life by 3 days compared to the control fruits.

Combination of paraffin waxing (3 per cent) of melting point of 75-80°C along with heat treatment (52°C for 5-10 minutes) resulted in good quality fruit with extended storage life. Individual wrapping of the fruit with newspaper or tissue paper imparted uniform surface colour development, reduced shrinkage and checked the spread of pathogens. Hydrocooling at 12-15°C and holding for 2 weeks at 15°C followed by storage for one week at ambient temperatures result in good quality fruits for a long time. After harvesting before cold storage treatments with salicylic acid @ 2mM lowers weight losses, fruit softening, disease incidence, pectin methylesterace and polygalactouronase activity in cv. Chausa, which ultimately results into alleviating chilling injury in mango. The ripening in mango cv. Alphonso was a potently determent by 1-methylcyclopropene. It can increases shelf life of fruits by retarding biochemical changes and enhancing shelf life of fruits without losing quality during cold storage. The chemical and sensory properties of Alphonso mango fruits were maintained by the treatment of Cel-fresh, 0.18 per cent (1-MCP)-1 tablet/2M^3 under cold storage conditions.

Control of Postharvest Decay

Postharvest diseases reduce fruit quality and result in severe losses. Latent infections such as anthracnose (*Colletotrichum gloeosporioides*). Alternaria black spot (*Alternaria alternate*) and stem end rot (*Lasiodiplodia theobromae* or *Dothiorella dominicana* or *Botryosphaeria spp.*) are the predominant postharvest diseases that cause severe postharvest losses and affect fruit quality during the supply chain. Incidence of postharvest decay during the postharvest management practices occurs as a result of spores (inoculums) coming in contact with the fruits. The spores are dispersed in the air or by contact and take place when the conditions are suitable for germination and growth. Conditions that favour the activity of postharvest pathogens include the presence of high relative humidity (RH), warm temperature and nutrients from the fruit surface, mainly sugars. Fruit becomes susceptible to infection as it softens. During handing, packing and transportation operations, small openings in theskin or wounded areas on fruit surface become the ideal sites for these pathogens to gain entry to the fruit tissue. Stem-end rots are reported to cause significant losses in mango during transit and storage, especially when anthracnose is controlled completely. Anthracnose and stem-end rot pathogens infect during fruit development, harvesting or de latexing or de sapping procedures and continue to advance causing significant losses in storage. Susceptibility of mango fruit to postharvest diseases increases during storage due to a series of physiological changes occurring in the fruit favouring the establishment and colonization of the pathogen and also to environmental conditions. The quiescent infections in climacteric fruit are terminated with reduction of antifungal compounds (combination of 5-(12-ciheptadecenyl)) resorcinol and 5-pentadecylresorcinol (resorcinols), production of ethylene (the ripening hormone in plants) and due to the changes in nutritional and texture changes. Postharvest disease control begins in the field and involves cultural and chemical practices and cultivar selection. Generally, control of postharvest disease in mango is achieved by adopting proper preharvest and postharvest management practices such as strict orchard hygiene management, application of fungicides and temperature management during storage and shipping. Postharvest temperature management is important because postharvest diseases are favoured at temperatures above optimum.

Hot Water Treatment (HWT)

Heat treatments especially HWT are widely used in many countries for insect and decay control in mango. Mango exporting countries are in a position to regulate the treatment due to the specific guidelines enforced by the importing countries, such as the specific duration for disinfection of the specific pest. HWT as a decay control treatment is applied commercially in few countries due to its efficacy. Bagging of mango fruit before harvest and postharvest treatment for 10 min HWT (52-55°C) was reported to reduce the anthracnose infection by 83 per cent and stem-end rot by 100 per cent. The temperature and the duration of the treatment depend on the size or weight of the fruit, stage of maturity, cultivar type and growing conditions and type of disease. It is recommended to subject the fruit to HWT within 24 h after harvest. HWT technology was shown to increase profit as a result of lower damage and higher market value. On the other hand, it can be practiced by small and medium scale mango growers with compatible practices, easily adopted in the supply chain, applicable for health conscious consumers and environmentally friendly method.

Biocontrol Agents

Biological control using microbial antagonist could be used on its own or in combination with a reduced concentration of synthetic fungicides.

Use of Modified or Controlled Atmospheres (MA/CA)

Postharvest disease control via maintaining the host resistance can be improved by shipping or storing fruits under CA conditions with higher CO_2 atmospheres. Short storage life of the mango fruits becomes the major constrain especially when exporting mangoes to distant overseas markets. The use of MA/CA technology allows extending the storage life while retaining the overall quality. MA/CA with higher CO_2 and lower O_2 (than normal air atmosphere) can delay ripening by inhibiting the production of ethylene, delaying the biochemical activities associated with ripening such as; slowing down the changes in skin and flesh colour, flavour, aroma and texture (fruit softening) and promoting resistance to the attack of postharvest pathogens by increasing the concentration of antifungal compounds due to oxidative process. A reduced O_2 concentration of around 3-5 per cent and an elevated CO_2 concentration of 5-10 per cent are the suggested atmosphere compositions for a successful MA/CA system for mango fruits.

Mature mango fruits

↓

Harvesting

↓

Collection in plastic crates

↓

Transportation of crates to pack house

↓

Transportation of crates to pack house

↓

Removal of latex from the fruits by keeping them upside down for a hours

↓

Grading

↓

Washing in solution of fungicide (for 2 minutes)

↓

Rinsing in ordinary water and drying with dry muslin cloth

↓

Application of food grade edible sugar (approved by the European Economic Community and USA for export)

↓

Removal of additional wax with muslin cloth

↓

Packing

↓

Carrying to cooling house

↓

Forced Air Cooling

↓

Lidding

↓

Palletization

↓

Transportation to cold storage

↓

Transportation to Dock Yard-Shipping

↓

Shipping

Use of fungicide wax emulsion containing 5 per cent orthophenyl phenol is reported to extend shelf-life in Alphonso by reducing respiration and delaying ripening of fruits. The addition of MH (1000-1500 ppm) to the emulsion further reduces the ripening rate and extends shelf-life. A hand operated wax-emulsion applicators should be used on a small scale but for large scale handling of fruits, power-operated applicators are also available. Storage of fruits of Alphonso at 8.3-10.0°C and Raspuri at 5.6-7.2°C in 7.5 per cent CO_2 atmosphere extends storage life to 35 and 49 days, respectively. Gamma rays irradiation (25 kRad) of 25-50 per cent ripe fruit of Haden kills stone weevil but did not extend shelf-life.

Postharvest Handling and Storage

Low Temperature Storage

Low temperature storage cannot be utilized to its full potential, in extending storage life of mango fruits because it is susceptible to chilling injury (CI) when stored at < 13°C. The most common visual symptoms of CI in fruits are dark colouration of the skin, prominence of lenticels, uneven ripening, development of off flavour and poor fruit quality. Mango fruit can be safely stored at 12-13°C for 2-3 weeks depending upon cultivars and harvest maturity except 'Dashehari' and 'Langra' at 7-8°C. Mature unripe fruit are generally more sensitive to CI, when stored at low temperature than ripe ones. The varying degree of amelioration of CI in mango fruit has been achieved using hot water treatment, intermittent warming, heat treatment, modified and controlled atmosphere storage and cold-shock treatment. The exogenous application of methyl jasmonate, ethrel, polyamines, oxalic or salicylic acid and 2-4-dichlorophenoxy acetic acid and postharvest application of 10-40 μL L-1 nitric oxide reduced CI in mango fruit. Taste, flavour and nutritional quality of ripe mango fruit have been reported to be affected by cold storage temperature and duration. 'Alphonso' mangoes stored at 10°C for 30 days resulted in poor flavour and reduced carotenoid levels at ripe stage. Generally, the safe storage temperature is pre-requisite to attain acceptable taste, flavour and nutritional value particularly bioactive compounds in the ripe fruits.

Controlled Atmosphere (CA) Storage

CA storage offers an attractive alternative to other methods in extending shelf life, maintaining fruit quality and enables long distance export of fruits using sea freight. This technique usually involves storing the fruit in an atmosphere comprised of reduced concentration of oxygen (O_2) and elevated carbon dioxide (CO_2) usually mixed with nitrogen, at optimum temperature and relative humidity. CA suppresses rate of respiration and ethylene production in the mango fruit, both during storage and ripening periods. Some limitations of mango CA include poor colour development, modification in the metabolism of some organic acids, alteration in texture, formation of undesirable flavour and odours, development of physiological disorders, high establishment, maintenance and operational costs as well as health and safety issues. The first report of mango storage at CA containing 9.2 per cent O_2 to prolong their ripening period dates back to 1937. The composition of O_2 and CO_2 gases in CA required for extending storage life of mango fruit varied among cultivars, cv. 'Alphonso' 5 per cent O_2 and 5 per cent CO_2; 'Banganapalli' (5 per cent O_2 and 3 per cent CO_2;). CA composition during storage influenced fruit colour development, softening, concentrations of sugars and organic acids, vitamins and carotenoids. Tree ripe 'Chausa' mango fruit can be successfully stored for two weeks using CA containing 3 per cent O_2 and 6 per cent CO_2 at 10°C. CA storage influences the nutritional quality of mango fruits. Hot water treated 'Alphonso' mango fruits (55°C for 5 min) followed by CA storage (5 per cent O_2 + 5 per cent CO_2) and ripened at ambient temperature showed highest carotenoid levels as compared to the fruit stored in normal atmosphere.

The effects of CA storage on the concentration of bioactive compounds with nutraceutical properties in ripe mango fruits in different cultivars are to be investigated. The effects of CA storage on production of aroma volatiles compounds in ripe fruits have been extensively studied in various mango cultivars. Aroma volatile production in CA stored ripe fruits has been reported to be influenced by cultivar, harvest fruit maturity, composition of CA, storage temperature and period. The CA comprised of reduced concentrations of O_2 and elevated levels of CO_2 also leads to anaerobic respiration and poor quality of ripe mango. CA storage comprised of CO_2 (> 6 per cent) and O_2 (> 2 per cent) induced anaerobic respiration and led to development of off-flavour and increased the concentration of acetaldehyde, ethanol and some esters in mangoes. In general, CA storage reduces production of aroma volatile compounds in ripe mango fruits. CA is beneficial in minimizing or preventing chilling injury in mango fruit and maintaining quality.

CA and Postharvest Disinfestations

The mango fruits are highly susceptible to various diseases during storage and ripening, such as anthracnose, stem-end rot and *Alternaria* rot. Anthracnose

(*Colletotrichum gloeosporioides* (Penz.) and Sacc.) and stem-end rot (*Dothiorella dominicana* Petrak and Cif and *Lasiodiplodia theobromae* have been known to cause highest losses during postharvest phase. Various pre-and postharvest approaches such as application of fungicides, biological antagonists and heat treatments alone and combined with fungicides have been tested to control postharvest diseases of mango fruits. Additionally, environmental hazards, safety concerns, health risks and consumer concerns regarding the use of fungicides offer attractive opportunities to develop alternative control measures such as natural means of postharvest disease control and storage environment. In general, CA treatment in combination with hot water treatment or fungicides are more effective in suppressing and delaying development of postharvest diseases in different cultivars of mango as compared to CA only.

Hypobaric Storage

Hypobaric storage (low pressure storage) is a form of CA storage. Produce is stored in a partial vacuum and chamber is vented continuously with water-saturated air to maintain oxygen levels and minimize water loss. The reduced partial pressure of oxygen in hypobaric storage retards ethylene action and production and ripening in some fruits. Hypobaric storage seems to be promising in extending shelf life of mango cultivars, ameliorating CI and reducing development of anthracnose and stem-end rot. Hypobaric storage has also been reported to be an effective treatment in controlling tephritid fruit by species. Hypobaric chambers are expensive to construct because of the low internal pressures required, which tends to limit the application of hypobaric storage to high-value produce.

Modified Atmosphere Packaging (MAP)

MAP involves the use of polymeric films to create a modified atmosphere that is high in CO_2 and low O_2 around the fruits. There is a large range of polymeric films available in the market with greater flexibility in gas permeability. Fruits are stored in sealed polythene film (40 μm thick low density polyethylene) bags at a suitable temperature. The fruits are removed from the bag to achieve normal ripening. MAP delays mango fruit ripening mainly due to increased levels of CO_2 and reduced concentrations of O_2, which reduce respiration rate and inhibit ethylene production. The plastic film also acts as a barrier to minimize water loss from the fruits. MAP is not commercially used in postharvest handling and shipment of mangoes because selection of a suitable MAP film is strongly influenced by cultivar, ripeness stage, weight and volume, thickness of film, perforation, permeability to moisture, O_2, CO_2, C_2H_4 and storage temperature and duration. Some newer films overcome the risks associated with MAP and are marketed as 'smart' or 'active' packaging. Micro-perforated film packaging overcomes some of these defects including off-flavours. The plastic films used for MAP creates an environmental hazard. Currently, there is a demand for biodegradable and ecofriendly packaging films to replace synthetic packaging films.

Edible Coatings

Application of edible coating forms a transparent film on the fruit surface, acts as a barrier to water and gases (O_2 and CO_2), imparts gloss, better colour, reduces fruit weight loss, extends storage life and minimize microbial spoilage. Edible coatings offer an attractive alternative to film packaging due to their environment-friendly characteristics. Semi-permeable coatings increase a fruit's skin resistance to gas diffusion, modify its internal atmosphere composition and depress its respiration rate. It can also create a modified atmosphere (MA) around the fruit similar to Ca storage but the changes in concentrations of O_2 and CO_2 are dependent on temperature and humidity. The performance of different types of edible coatings are dependent on their composition and genotype. Various types of coatings such as carnauba wax, shellac, zein, cellulose derivatives, chitosan and its derivatives and other composite mixtures containing sucrose esters of fatty acids and a sodium salt of carboxymethyl cellulose have been tested to extend storage life of mango fruits with variable results.

The natural edible coatings in fresh mangoes are preferred over the petroleum based waxes, which are banned in some countries. 'Kensington Pride' mango fruit coated with Mango Carnauba wax exhibited significantly improved fruit aroma volatiles including total aroma volatiles, monoterpenes, sesquiterpenes and aldehydes while maintaining comparative aromatic and lactone concentrations and reducing total alcohol levels compared to the control fruits. Edible coating seems promising in extending storage life of mangos.

Grading

The fruits are checked prior to packing to ensure the absence of blemishes, bruises and insects and mechanical injuries. Fruits should be graded in each carton according to variety, size by weight or diameter and the extent of maturity. Minimum weight and size specifications are kept into consideration as per the market requirement. After waxing, fruits are packed in four kg corrugated fiber board (CFB) cartons with vents on both sides. The ideal size of box is 40 × 27.5 × 10.0 cm. The height of the box may be adjusted as per height of the fruits. The box should indicate weight, variety, count and category of the fruit with proper labeling. The counts with the fruit weight (+/- 30 grams) used as a guideline for a 4 kilogram carton are 6 fruits (666 g each), 8 fruits (500 g), 10 fruits (400 g), 12 fruits (330 g), 14 fruits (290 g) and 16 fruits (250 g).

Table 15: Criteria and Description of Grades (According to Agmark standards), Mangoes are Classified into following Classes

Grade Designations	*Grade Requirements*	*Grade Tolerances*
1	*2*	*3*
Extra class	Mangoes must be of superior quality. They must be characteristic of the cultivar. They must be free of defects, with the exception of very slight superficial defects, provided these do not affect the general appearances of the produce, the quality, the keeping quality and presentation in the package.	5 per cent by number or weight of mangoes not satisfying the requirements for the grade but meeting those of Class I or exceptionally, coming within the tolerances of that grade.

Grade Designations	*Grade Requirements*	*Grade Tolerances*
Class I	Mangoes must be of good quality. They must be characteristic of the cultivars. Mangoes may have following slight defects, provided these do not affect the general appearance of the produce, the quality, the keeping quality and presentation in the package. - slight defects in shape; - slight skin defects due to rubbing or sunburn, suberized stains due to resin exudation (elongated trails included) and healed bruises not exceeding 2, 3, 4, 5 sq. cm. for size groups A, B, C, D, respectively.	10 per cent by number or weight of mangoes not satisfying the requirements for the grade but meeting those of Class II grade or, exceptionally coming within the tolerances of that grade.
Class II	This grade includes mangoes which do not qualify for inclusion in the higher grades but satisfy the minimum requirements. Mangoes may have following defects, provided they retain their essential characteristics as regards the quality, keeping quality and presentation. - defects in shape, slight skin defects due to rubbing or sunburn, suberized stains due to resin exudation (elongated trails included) and healed bruises not exceeding 4, 5, 6, 7 sq. cm. for size groups A, B, C, D, respectively.	10 per cent by number or weight of mangoes not satisfying the requirements of the grade but meeting the minimum requirements.

Provision Concerning Size

Table 16: Size is Determined by the Weight of the Fruits

Size Code	*Weight in Grams (minimum)*	*Maximum Permissible difference between Fruits within the Package (in grams)*
A	100-200	50
B	201-350	75
C	351-550	100
D	551-800	125

Packaging

Recent technologies advancement and improvements in logistics have increased the fresh mango trade manifold both in remote domestic markets of its growing countries and global markets. Supermarkets in the advanced countries are now offering mangoes round the year due to difference in its seasonality. However, delivering quality with consistency is the great challenge in mango marketing and the role of appropriate packaging is one of the most crucial aspect of mango logistics. The term right packaging is relevant to particular supply chain (air, sea, road) and intended markets; however, the very basic requirement remains proper fruit containment, protection, communication and convenience in distribution and marketing along with their positive impact on quality and shelf life of fruits. The proper packaging of graded fruits is done to maintain quality. Perforated cardboard boxes are being used for packaging purpose. In these boxes, individually wrapped fruits with tissue paper are packed or paper shreds are used as cushioning material. Mangoes can successfully be stored for 2 to 3 weeks by following recommended harvesting practices and proper postharvest handling and storage. Stickers are used for proper identification. The fruits of cv. Dashehari stored in open condtion decomposed after 10 days of storage, whereas, the fruits in polyfilm remained fresh even after 14 days of storage with low physiological weight loss (15 per cent) and maintained higher firmness (0.8 kg/cm^2) and TSS (18.69°Brix) make its marketing easy. The level of polygalacturonase activitiy retarded from 0.146 to 0.095 U/ml in polybag, while it increased from 0.146 to 0.268 U/ml in fruits stored under open condition. Polybag is effective in prolonging the shelf-life of mango cv. Dashehari fruits by way of its ability to maintain fruit firmness and delaying the ripening process.

Table 17: Details of Wooden Boxes in which Mangoes are Packed in Domestic Market

Type of Carton	*Inner Dimension (cm)*	*Capacity (kgs)*
Wooden crates	45 × 30 × 30 (Ratnagiri)	16-18
	21.6 × 21.6 × 42 (Malihabad)	10-11
However, Alphonso and Kesar are packed in CFB boxes.		

For Export the Postharvest Manual for Export of Mangoes, APEDA, New Delhi had decided norms for packaging are as follows:

- ☆ Each individual fruit of mango will be enclosed in a clean, white, soft, expandable and netted type of polystyrene sleeve to prevent bruising before packing in a box.
- ☆ The mangoes must be packed in insect-proof boxes. If ventilated boxes are used, all the ventilator openings of the box should be covered with insect-proof screen and all the sides of box should be sealed with adhesive tape to prevent any entry of pests.
- ☆ The materials used inside the package must be new, clean and of a quality such as to avoid causing any external or internal damage to the produce.
- ☆ The use of materials, particularly of paper or stamps bearing trade specifications is allowed, provided the printing or labeling has been done with non-toxic ink or glue.

Mangoes shall be packed in each container in compliance with the recommended International Code of Practice for Packaging and Transport of Fresh Fruits and Vegetables (CAC/RCP44-1995, Amd.1-2004).

Table 18: Specification details for Corrugated Fibre Board (CFB) Boxes for Packing Mangoes for Exports

Sl.No.		Ring and Flap (4 kg)	Full Telescopic (4 kg)	Ring Flap (8 kg)	Full Telescopic (8 kg)
1.	Material of construction	3 Ply Corrugated fibre board	3 Ply Corrugated fibre board	5 Ply Corrugated fibre board	5 Ply Corrugated fibre board
2.	Grammage (g/msq), Min (outer to inner)	*230/140/140	*230*140/140	*230/140/140	*230/140/140
3.	Bursting strength kg/cm sq. Min	6.50	6.50	10.50	6.50
4.	Puncture resistance, ozs cms/tear cms Min	110	110	280	110
5.	Compression strength, kgf, Min	275	275	250	250
6.	Cobb (30 minutes) g/m sq, Max	130	130	130	130

* Outer ply of duplex board.

Distribution of Produce from Primary to Terminal Market

- Mangoes grown in different parts of the country are transported to the big cities for marketing.
- The fruits produced in Andhra Pradesh and Tamil Nadu find markets in Nagpur, Bombay and Calcutta.
- The important wholesale mango markets in India are Calcutta, Delhi, Bombay, Madras, Ahmedabad, Pune and Nagpur.
- Mangoes for these big markets are usually collected at the central places in all the mango growing areas, *e.g.* in Uttar Pradesh, Lucknow and Varanasi; in Gujarat, Gandevi, Gadat and Amalsar talukas and in Maharashtra, Ratnagiri and Vengurla.

Delhi and Bombay are the most important markets for dispatch of mangoes. At Delhi all the mangoes are assembled at Sabzimandi, Ashoka market and at Bombay at Crawford and Byculla markets for distribution.

*(Source: Postharvest Manual for Export of Mangoes, APEDA, New Delhi.)

Transportation to Pack House

The collection centres near the farm with basic facilities for desapping, sorting and washing would help to sort out the quality fruits to be transported to the pack houses. The harvested fruits kept in crates are transported to the pack house carefully by clean vehicles, preferably refrigerated ones without exposing them to the sun to avoid damage or injury to the fruits. The pack house should have basic facilities including a roof, clean floor, water source, desapping bench, sorting/ grading tables, size grader and roller conveyor, wash tanks, automatic washing system and hot water (52°C for 5-10 minutes) and vapour heat treatment (46°C for 20-30 minutes) equipments to control anthracnose and fruit fly, respectively. Desapping is done immediately after harvest, otherwise, the initial spurt of sap will burn the fruit peel, leaving a blemish that will develop during storage and transport reduces the quality and marketability of fruits. Sapburn injury in mango is regarded as the most serious problem as it reduces the aesthetic appeal and down grade the fruit quality with considerable economic losses. Clip the fruit stalk while holding the fruit with stem end down. Place fruit on desapping bench or specially knitted pallets and allow them to drain sap for 20 to 30 minutes until the sap flow is stopped. A fine water spray over the fruit or dipping fruits in water containing wetting agent reduces the risk of sap burn. Desapping can also be carried out in the field or at the collection centres.

For the control of sapburn injury, physiologically mature mango fruits of cv. Chausa were destemmed and treated with different desapping agent solutions [calcium ydroxide (1 per cent), sodium hydroxide (1 per cent), alum (0.5 and 1 per cent)] by dipping them for 5 min immediately after harvesting, fruits. After treatment application, fruits were air-dried and stored at ambient condition (30 ± 2°C) for 12 days. Fruits desapped with sodium hydroxide (1 per cent) showed significantly lower (7.6-fold) sapburn injury followed by alum (0.5 per cent) treatment than control. Respiration and ethylene evolution rates were also significantly suppressed and delayed with sodium hydroxide (1 per cent) treatment. Fruit quality parameters like colour, total soluble solids, titratable acidity and total sugars content were found higher in calcium hydroxide and sodium hydroxide treated fruits than control and alum treated fruits. Fruits are washed properly to remove any latex stains, spray residues and sooty moulds. For this, a solution with water and detergent are required. The fruits are washed with this solution by rubbing gently with soft muslin cloth. Washed fruits are then rinsed in clean water and wiped with dry muslin cloth or air dried to remove surface moisture. Fruits pass under a spray washer and onto a moving conveyor belt for size grading. Fungicide treatment, either separately or included in the hot water bath also reduces the infection. The fungicide to be used will depend on exporting and importing country regulations.

Storage and Ripening

Usually the green and mature fruits store well than those harvested ripe from the tree. Under normal conditions (25-30°C), mango has a storage life ranging from 4 to 16 days after harvesting. Storage of mangoes at low temperature (13°C) may increase its storage life to 28 to 45 days. Due to the short postharvest life of tropical fruits like mango, precooling is an important postharvest unit operation. There are several techniques commercially employed such as hydrocooling, mechanical cooling augmented by liquid nitrogen, air cooling. The precooling process should be as fast as possible but the cooling should not result in any chilling injury to the fruit. Liquid nitrogen has high cooling capacity and due to the inertness of the vaporized nitrogen gas is very much applicable for precooling purposes. Its boiling point is – 195.6°C. This severe cold temperature raises concerns on the possibility of chilling injury to the fruit. Other common precooling techniques for mangoes are hydrocooling and air cooling with mechanical refrigeration. It has been observed that all the commercial cooling techniques, such as hydrocooling, air cooling have comparable effect on the overall quality as measured through some of the physicochemical parameters such as firmness, aroma. However, it has also been observed that liquid nitrogen augmented air cooling technique has some edge over other conventional commercial cooling in terms of time required for cooling.

Before storage, the fruits should be pre-cooled. Forced air precooling system has been found the most efficient for fresh fruits. At harvest, the temperature of the fruits may vary from 25-35°C depending on the locality, month and time of harvest. The forced air precooling makes it possible to bring down the temperature to 12.5-13.5°C in about six hours which is recommended temperature for storage/shipment of mango. High humidity of 85-95 per cent is desirable right from the pre-cooled boxes are palletized in wooden pallets. Thereafter, pallets with boxes on them are either shifted to cold storage or brought to the dock yards by refrigerated vans for transshipment in refrigerated containers. Mango cultivars Dashehari, Mallika, Amrapali and Pusa Arunima store well at 12°C, Langra at 14°C and Chausa at 8°c with 85 per cent to 90 per cent relative humidity. Dashehari mangoes dipped in 4$ solution of calcium chloride at sub atmospheric pressure of 500 mm Hg for 5 minutes store for 27 days at 12°C temperature.

Ripening

Mango is a climacteric fruit and characterized by a series of physiological and biochemical changes that occur during ripening, which are initiated by autocatalytic production of ethylene and increase in rate of respiration. In mango, ethylene rises after climacteric burst in respiration. Ethylene production in unripe fruits is very low and almost undetectable during fruit development and maturation and appears upon initiation of ripening. Ethylene, even at very low concentration (0.01 ppm) can trigger the ripening process in mango. Respiration patterns and the amount of ethylene released vary among cultivars, under different climatic conditions. In 'Alphonso', respiration burst is seen on day 5 after harvest with an ethylene production of 0.02-0.18 ppm, while in 'Kent' and 'Haden', it occurs on days 9 and 11, respectively with an ethylene production of 0.08-3.0 ppm (Burg and Burg, 1962). The concentration of ethylene released is comparatively higher in some cultivars, *i.e.* 5-8 ppm in 'Amrapali' and 'Dashehari' mangoes compared to others.

Exogenous ethylene treatment to mango increases its autocatalytic production. The amount of ethylene released higher than that from non treated fruits, whereas, fruit treatment with ethylene perception inhibitors such as 1-methylcyclopropene (1-MCP) reduces endogenous production and delays ripening in cultivar 'Dashehari'. Ethylene biosynthesis decreases when fruits are stored at low temperature in controlled atmosphere particularly reduced levels of oxygen. This change in ethylene production is due to altered activity of ACS and ACO by external factors. Exogenous application of ethephon to fruits during ripening increased respiration rate, ethylene production and fatty acids content in fruits, whereas, ethylene action inhibitors such as aminoethoxyvinylglycine (AVG) and 1-MCP suppressed rate of respiration and ethylene production. Similarly, the exogenous application of ethephon increased the production of total aroma volatiles, monoterpenes, sesquiterpenes, aldehydes, total esters, alcohols and tetradecane. These volatiles were reduced in AVG and 1-MCP treated fruits. Mango ACS and ACO genes have been identified and enzyme activites correlated with respective transcripts, which were undetectable in unique fruits and reached their peak during complete ripening. Exogenous NO application to mango fruits delays climacteric rise in ethylene production and reduces respiration rate. Most developmental and adaptive processes in plants including ripening result from a complex interaction between two or more hormones. Besides ethylene, other hormones such as auxins, abscisic acid, jasmonic acid, brassinosteriods and polyamines play a vital role in ripening but a complete understanding of the hormonal control of ripening is lacking because of insufficient data on their endogenous levels during various conditions.

Ripening Related Changes in Mango

Mango fruits are characterized by their highly divergent and specific aesthetic qualities such as complex/delicate aroma, pleasant taste, exotic colours, succulence, flavour and texture which make these attractive and edible. These changes generally include modification of cell wall ultra-structure and texture (softening), conversion of starch to sugars (gluconeogenesis), variation in pH, change in pigmentation, development of colour and accumulation of flavours and aroma. Besides these, ripening imparts many qualities and nutritional characteristics to fruits that play a vital role in human health and nutrition.

Textural Changes during Ripening

During fruit softening, cell walls are modified by solubilisation, de-esterification and de-polymerization, accompanied by an extensive loss of neutral sugars and galacturonic acid. This is followed by solubilisation of the remaining sugars residues and oligosaccharides. The major classes of cell wall polysaccharides that undergo modifications during ripening are pectins, cellulose and hemicelluloses. Starch is another major polysaccharide present in mango and its enzymatic hydrolysis results in pronounced loosening of cell structure with development of sweetness due to sugar accumulation. In cultivars 'Alphonso', polysaccharides like starch, pectin, cellulose and hemicelluloses content decrease from unripe to ripe stage with concomitant increase in soluble sugars. Fruit softening is characterized by increased solubility of cell wall pectins, which are cultivar-related. Several pecin-degrading and modifying enzymes such as *exo-* and *endo-*polygalacturonases (PGs), pectate lyases (PLs), pectin methylesterase (PMEs), β-galactosidases (β -Gals) and α- arabinofuranosidases (Arabfs) may act synergistically within the cell wall to reduce the apparent molecularize of pectic polymers leading to the depolymerization and increased solubility of pectic polysaccharides. Cellulase enzyme activitiy in several Indian mango cultivars such 'Alphonso', 'Badami' and 'Totapuri' increased during ripening. Arabinanase, galactanase and mannanase are prominent enzymes in mango fruits and their activity peaks at climacteric stage of ripening

Changes in Mango Peel and Pulp Colour

Colour changes in mango fruits are due to the disappearance of chlorophyll and appearance of other pigments. Chlogoplasts are transformed to chromoplasts

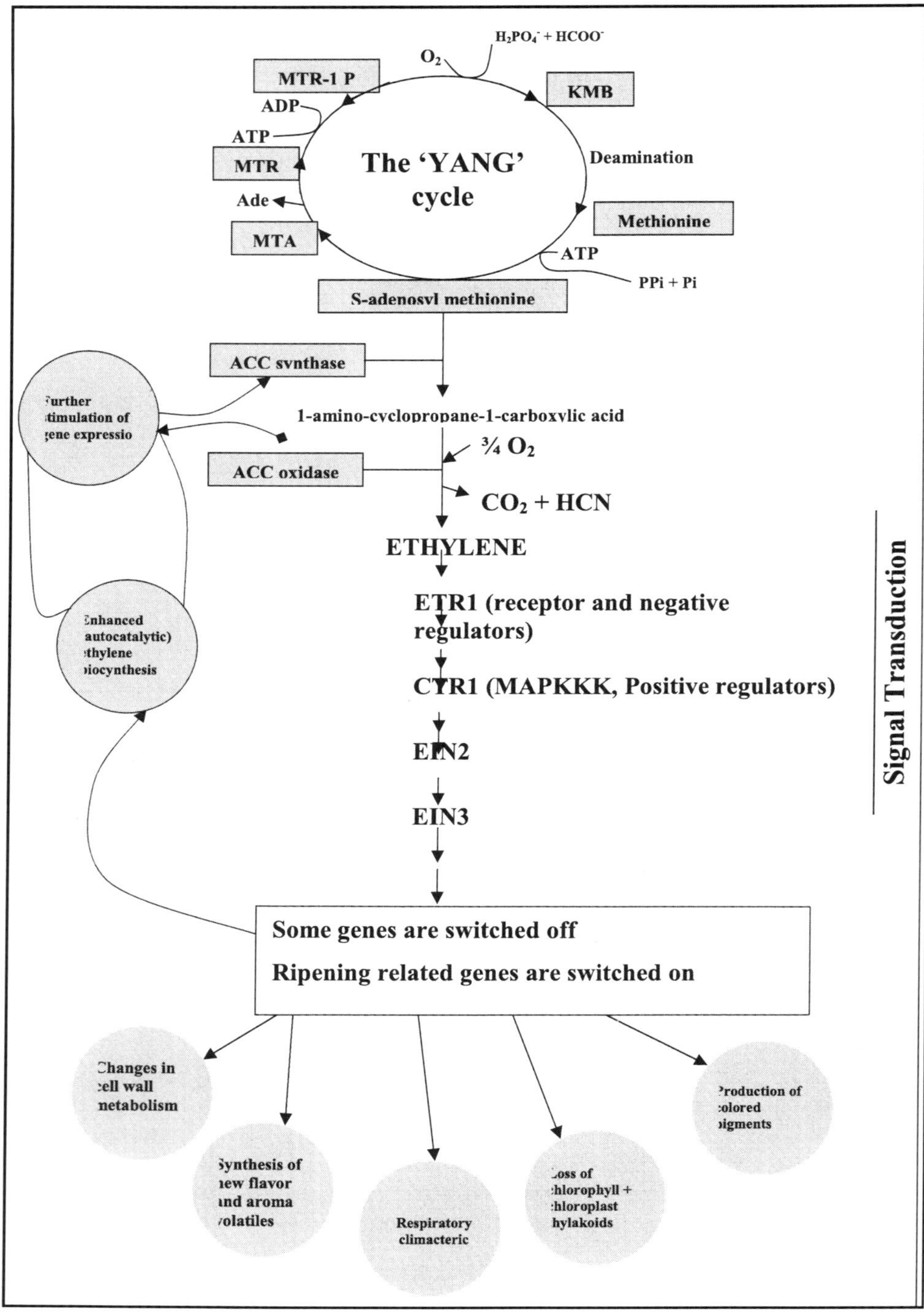

$H_2PO_4^- + HCOO^-$
O_2
MTR-1 P
KMB
ADP
ATP
MTR
The 'YANG' cycle
Deamination
Ade
Methionine
MTA
ATP
PPi + Pi
S-adenosyl methionine
ACC synthase
Further stimulation of gene expressio
1-amino-cyclopropane-1-carboxylic acid
¾ O_2
ACC oxidase
CO_2 + HCN
ETHYLENE
ETR1 (receptor and negative regulators)
CTR1 (MAPKKK, Positive regulators)
EIN2
EIN3
Signal Transduction
Enhanced (autocatalytic) ethylene biocynthesis
Some genes are switched off
Ripening related genes are switched on
Changes in cell wall metabolism
Synthesis of new flavor and aroma volatiles
Respiratory climacteric
Loss of chlorophyll + chloroplast thylakoids
Production of colored pigments

Figure 6

containing yellow or red pigments. Different types of anthocyanins and carotenoids such as β-carotene, xanthophylls esters, xanthophylls and lycopene are synthesized and accumulate in the vacuole. Changes in fruit colour during ripening vary among fruits depending on the compound formed during ripening. Depending on the cultivar and pigment accumulation, skin colour can change from dark green to olive; sometimes reddish, orange-yellow or yellowish. Some cultivars develop a reddish blush, which has been attributed to anthocyanins. Mango fruit pulp contains high concentrations of carotenoids (up to 9 mg 100 g^{-1}), causes the development of an intense yellow to orange colour. In yellow cultivars, carotenoids and xanthophylls are the predominant pigments, whereas, anthocyanins occur in the skin of some cultivars. The most abundant carotene of mango is *all-trans-carotene*, while the most important xanthophylls are violaxanthin and its isomers.

Changes in Taste, Aroma and Flavour during Mango Ripening

Fruit flavour depends upon taste (balance between sweetness and sourness or acidity and low to on astringency) and aroma (concentrations of odour-active volatile compounds). Although, taste and aroma are well integrated in their contribution to the overall flavour, aroma is often considered to play a dominant role in flavour. Taste development is due to a general increase in sweetness, which is the result of increased gluconeogenesis, hydrolysis of polysaccharides, especially starch, decreased acidity and accumulation of sugars and organic acids resulting in an excellent sugar/acid blend. Sweetness is determined by the concentrations of predominant sugars mainly fructose, sucrose and glucose. Sourness is determined by the concentrations of the predominant organic acids, which are citric acid, malic acid and tartaric acid. Some amino acids, such as aspartic and glutamic acid may also contribute to sourness. Several factors affect sugar and acid contents in mango, including cultivars, stage of maturity at harvest, postharvest treatments and storage conditions. Uniform ripening in mango can be induced with treatment of ethrel (62.5-185.7 ml/100 litres water) at 52°C for 5 minute. The concentration of ethrel varies according to the stage of fruit maturity. Mango fruit picked at mature-green stage exposed to 20-100 µL L-1 ethylene for 24 h at 21°C and 95 per cent RH had univorm and rapid ripening. Cultivars Dashehari, Chausa and Langra fruits harvested at physiological maturity were exposed to 100 ppm ethylene for 24 hours at 24°C, 95 per cent relative humidity for 8 days. Dashehari reached optimum eating maturity on 4th day and unable to further storage, whereas, the Langra and Chausa ripened at 6th day and last for 8th day. Response of the cultivars were different, ethylene evolution rate was maximum in Dashehari (1.81 µl C_2H_4 kg^{-1} h^{-1}) and minimum in Langra (0.40 µl C_2H_4 kg^{-1} h^{-1}) on 4th day of storage. Climacteric peak was declined on 8th day and lowest peak was recorded in Langra (0.31 µl C_2H_4 kg^{-1} h^{-1}) followed by Chausa.

Processing

Mangoes are utilized at all stages of its growth and development in the form of processed products. For instance, delicious product like panna, pickles, aamchur, chutaney and so on are prepared from raw fruits and refreshing products like juice, nectar, squash, pulp, aampapad, slices in brine *etc.* from the ripe fruits. Dashehari and Amrapali are suitable for nectar making. Alphonso, Kesar and Pairi are most suitable cultivars for preparation of mango pulp. Mango fruits contains 10-20 per cent sugar and are an important source of vitamins, besides vitamin B and C. They have rich, luscious aromatic flavour. Young and unripe fruits are acidic and seed kernel contains edible fat. Sindura, Mallika and Totapuri cultivars had significantly different physico-chemical and compositional characterstics. Sindura cultivar had a characteristic red colour in the peel with high carotenoid content and slightly lower pulp content. Mallika contained higher pulp content with a pale yellow colour in the peel and higher total soluble solids. Totapuri contained slightly lower pulp content than Mallika, lower total soluble solids and lower carotenoids among the cultivars. Sindura and Mallika pulps had significantly higher viscosity than Totapuri. Processing of the pulps resulted in significant decrease of carotenoids irrespective of the cultivar. Sensory quality of canned mango slices showed higher acceptability for Mallika followed by Sindura and Totapuri. Mango nectar prepared from Sindura was highly acceptable followed by Totapuri and Mallika. Sindura and Mallika are used for processing into nectar, juice beverages and slices, which will result in value addition to these underutilized mango cultivars.

Pickles

Mature raw mangoes are used for making pickles with oil. For making pickles in oil, one kilogram of small slices are mixed with 40g salt, 50g fenugreek seeds, 50g ginger, 25g turmeric, 25g red chilli, 35g of black pepper and 30g fennel dipped in 300 ml oil. This pickle is the filled in clean glass jars and cured in the sun for a few days. For oil less pickle, the peeled fruits are sliced into small pieces and mixed with 2 per cent salt, 8 per cent chilli power and 1.5 per cent asafetida on the weight basis. The pickle is then cured in sun for few days by stirring, filled in clean glass jars and kept in clean and dry place.

Aamchur

Aamchur is prepared by grinding slices collected from raw, healthy and clean fruit. Peeled mature or immature green mango slices are dipped in 1.5 per cent to 2.0 per cent solution of potassium metabisulphite for 5-10 minutes. After draining the slices are kept in stainless steel or aluminium trays, dried in the sun or solar drier, reduced to 4 per cent in weight, ground into powder and stored in air tight containers.

Slices

Slices are made from peeled mature or immature green, clean and healthy fruits dipped in the 1.5 per cent potassium metabisulphite solution for 5 minutes, dried and mixed with equal amount of salt. Thesse slices are stored in polythene pouches and later used for the preparation of products after washing salt. Slices are also prepared from the ripe mangoes by cutting 1-2 cm thick slice. These slices are transferred to the boiling syrup containing 40-45 per cent sugar, 3.5 per cent citric acid and 350 ppm sulphur dioxide (0.7 g KMS per litre water) for 5 minutes. The slices 500-550g are filled in clean jars and the boiling 40° Brix syrup 450-500g is poured over slices. The jars are then covered by lids sealed with wax and stored in dry place.

Canning of Mango Pulp

Pulp was analysed for total soluble solids, pH and acidity. The pulp was blended with 10 per cent water for improving the flow characteristics and facilitating heat transfer during canning process. pH of the mango pulp was adjusted to 4 by the addition of 10 per cent citric acid solution (w/v). Pulp was heated to 85°C in a stainless steel steam jacketed kettle and filled hot into sterilized A 2 ½ open top sanitary (OTS) tin containers with a net weight of 850g. The cans were sealed and processed in boiling water bath for 20 minutes and cooled in running tap water. Cooled cans were wiped, labelled and stored at room temperature.

Beverages

Baverages are prepared from raw and ripe mangoes. Beverages from raw mangoes (panna or pana) is prepared by roasting or boiling mangoes with equal amount of water and extracting the pulp in mixer. The constituents of this beverage included one kg of extract of pulp, 1.6 kg each of sugar and water, 75g of salt, 25g mint, 15g cumin, 4.5g black pepper and 20g citric acid. This mixed material is heated to 95°C and filled in clean glass bottles. This is the raw mango squash, which is a modified version of 'Panna'. The only difference is that sugar is not used in 'panna' and whole boiled or roasted mango is consumed after filtration through muslin cloth. The beverages prepared from ripe mangoes are juice and nectar. In the case of juice, with each kg of pulp, two litres water, 350g sugar and 6-8g citric acid are added. The total soluble soids content are made upto 15 per cent by adding sugar and acidity to 0.3 per cent by adding citric acid. This mixture is heated to 95°C, filled hot in clean and sterile bottles and put with crown cork. After sterilizing in boiling water for 10-15 minutes, the bottles are stored in cool dry place after cooling to room temperatures. In nectar, the pulp content is maintained to the level of 15 per cent but the method of preparation is similar. For each kilogramme of pulp, 5 litres water, 850g sugar and 15-20g citric acid are added.

Squash

In one kilogramme of fresh mango pulp, 1.8kg sugar is added after dissolving it in 1.21 litres of water and filtering for homogenizing the pulp with sugar syrup. This mixture is heated upto 78°C and mixed with 40grams citric acid and 3grams potassium metabisulphite after dissolving them in a little quantity of water. In stored pulp, 1.6kg pulp is mixed with, 1.7kg sugar and 30-40grams citric acid, potassium metabisulphite (KMS) is not added in this case. The squash so prepared is filled in sterilized bottle covered with crown cork and stored in cool dry place.

Mango Leather (Aam Papad)

Ripe mango pulp (6 kgs) is homogenized in a blender and citric acid (18 grams) and potassium metabisulphite (2.0-2.5 grams) dissolved in a small quantity of water are added and mixed thoroughly with the pulp. Pulp is spread to one centimeter thickness in stainless steel tray smeared with oil/butter and dried in solar drier and then again one centimeter thick pulp is spread on the dried layers. This is dried to about 8 per cent moisture level and then is cut into small pieces, packed in polythene pouches and stored in dry and cool place.

Jam

Ripe mango pulp (6 kgs) is homogenized in blender. Sugar (5 kgs) is mixed with pulp after dissolving it in water and filtering with muslin cloth and heated to its $3/4^{th}$ volume. Citric acid (18 grams) is mixed after dissolving in a little quantity of water to the boiling slurry. The jam is kept in wide mouthed sterilized jars, which are sealed with air tight lid.

Blends

Mango blends can be prepared by mixing other fruits like papaya (500 grams) or pear (100 grams) per kg of mango pulp. The specific quantities of water (7.5, 5.5 and 5.2 litres), sugar (1.25, 0.85 and 0.85 kg), citric acid (2.5, 18-19 and 18 grams) and Potassium metabisulphite (1.4, 1.0 and 1.0 gram) are added to the above blends. The pulp of blended fruits are homogenized with 50-60° Brix sugar syrup. Water is added and the mixture is heated 95° C. Citric acid is added after dissolving it in a little quantity of water. Potassium metabisulphite (0.7 g/kg) is added for storing more than 3 months. The beverage is filled in sterilized bottles and the sterilized (15 minutes in boiling water) crown cork is put on the mouth of bottles.

Flavoured Mango Pulp Concentrate

Two fold concentrate of mango pulp can be obtained by conventional evaporative concentration procedure. Aroma recovery is done during or before concentration procedure. Aroma recovery is done during or before concentration and this enables effective restoration of aroma to mango pulp. Juice concentrate and aroma concentrate can be mixed together to obtain flavoured concentrate.

Select ripe mangoes
↓
Cut into squares
↓
Extract pulp
↓
Pulverize it
↓
Aroma recovery
↓

Aroma concentrate	Stripped pulp concentrate
↓	↓

↓
Mix

Mango Fruit Bar

It is confectionery prepared by mixing mango with measured amount of sugar and other ingredients. Spread this on trays and dry in a drier, until moisture is reduced to the desired level. The dried sheet is cut into suitable size and is then packed.

Mango Toffee

For its preparation, mango pulp (puree) is mixed with sucrose, glucose, skim-milk powder and hydrogenated fat. The mixture is boiled in steam jacked kettle to reduce final weight. The product is spread on to the trays and allowed to dry in a drier. The dried sheet is cut into desirable sizes and packed.

Mango Waste Utilization

A number of products can be prepared from the peel. Good quality pectin can be prepared from it to be used for the preparation of jams and jellies. Pectin yield has been shown to be in the range of 10-16 per cent. Peel waste can also be used for alcohol and vinegar preparation. Mango aroma concentrate can be prepared from mango peel by steaming it, followed by successive evaporation of condensed mango peel. Aroma concentrate can be used for flavouring beverages and dairy products. The peel is also been shown to be a good source of carotenoid pigments.

Mango seed or stone content ranges from 9 to 23 per cent and the kernel content of the seed ranges from 46 to 73 per cent. The kernel is good source of fat, which ranges from 9to 16 per cent. India is the largest producer of mango in the world, contributing to nearly 46 per cent of the total world production. Despite all this mango processors of India are facing challenges including; middle men menace, huge postharvest loss, lack of support by the concerned nodal bodies, poor profitability and seasonality of the processing activity and so on leading to processing of just 2 per cent of total production. Major reasons for ill growth of this industry include: non availability of right cultivars are ideal for processing; lack of necessary infrastructure; lack of cooperative effort amongst processing community and lack of integration of all the activities starting from orchard gate till final consumers because of ill functioning of the government departments/nodal bodies/institutions with no clear direction and goals. A coordinated, integrated and strategic effort of all the stake holders is must to turn around this industry. Mango processing industry of India has to undergo a radical shift to address all the above constraints and reap the enormous benefits which this sector is to offer. Constraints have to be studied in wholesome, integrated and strategic manner rather than adopting piecemeal approach.

Glossary

Abaxial: The side of an organ turned away from the axis, for example, the under side of a leaf.

Aberrant: Different from the normal.

Abnormal: Different from the usual or prevailing form or structure.

Abortion: Failure of development or imperfect development.

Abortive: Imperfectly developed or underdeveloped.

Abruptly pinnate: Pinnate but without terminal leaflet.

Abscission: The shedding of some part or structure as a leaf or flower at its base that break apart readily.

Acaulescent: Apparently without a stem that is with the main stem underground and only basal leaves and slender, leafless flowering stems appearing above ground level.

Accessory: Additional beyond the normal; extra.

Accrescent: Increasing in size after flowering, enlarging with age.

Accumbent: Applied to cotyledons with their edges turned towards the main axis of the embryo.

Aceriform : Similar to the leaf of a maple.

Acerose: Needlelike.

Achene: A dry one seeded fruit with a firm close fitting wall which does not open by any regular dehiscence.

Achene beak: The persistent and hardened style of an achene.

Achlamydeous: Having neither calyx or corolla.

Acicular: Needle shaped and very slender.

Acorn: The leathery fruit of an oak, containing a single large seed and enclosed basally in a cup formed from bracts.

Actinomorphic: Radially symmetrical, that is, capable of division by straight boundaries into three or more similar sections.

Active bud: A growing bud.

Aculeate: Covered with prickles.

Acuminate: With a long, tapering point set off rather abruptly from the main body.

Acute: With a pointed end forming an acute angle, that is, less than a right angle.

Adaxial: On the side towards the axis, as for example,the upper side of a leaf.

Adherent: Grown fast to a structure of a different bind, as for example, a stamen grown fast to a petal.

Adnate: Adjective of Adnation.

Adnation : Fusion with or attachment to another structure from the beginning of development.

Adventitious: A structure occurring in an unusual position as, for example, an adventitious root formed from a stem or a leaf.

Adventitious bud: A bud produced in a unusual or unexpected place, as for example near the point of injury of a stem or on leaf or a root.

Adventitious roots: Are those shoots that arise from the aerial plant parts, underground stem or from old roots.

Adventitious shoots: Are those shoots that develop on roots or inter-nodally on stems.

Adventive: Said of an introduced plant beginning to spread into a new locality or region.

Aerial root: Roots exposed to the air, as those of tropical plants growing on the trees.

Aestival: Of the summer.

Aestivation: Arrangement of the young flower parts in the bud.

Agglomerate: Crowded into a dense cluster but not joined synonymus Aggregate.

Aitinomic: As referred to parthenocarpy, the ability of a part to develop parthenocarpic fruits only in response to some stimulus external to ovary.

Alate : With a wing.

Albumen: A deposit of reserve food material accompanying the embryo. Such reserves often are in the endosperm.

Alga: A seaweed or one of the essentially microscopic pond scums. Plural algae.

Alliaceous: Having the odor or taste of garlic or onions.

Alternate: With a single structure of each bind occurring at each level of the axis appearing to alternate on opposite sides of the axis, but actually in a spiral arrangement.

Alveolate: With angular depressions forming a pattern like honey comb.

Alveolus: A depression with in an alveolate pattern.

Ament: A soft, usually scaly spike of small, apetalous, unisexual flowers, this usually falling as a single unit.

Amentiferous: With the flowers in aments *i.e.* catkins.

Amorphous: With no definite form.

Amphitropous: Describing an ovule bent back along and adnate to the funiculus, but with the micropyle not bent all the way back to the funiculus.

Amplexicaul: Clasping the stem, that is, the base nearly surrounding it.

Ampliate: enlarged.

Anastomosing: Joining each other and forming a network, the term being applied to veins as the veins of the leaf.

Anatropous: Descriptive of an ovule in which the body is bent backward along the funiculus and adnate to it.

Ancipital: Two edged.

Androecium: The male reproductive organs; in the flowering plants the stamens- a collective term for all those within a flower.

Androgynous: A term applied to an inflorescence which includes both staminate and pistillate flowers, the staminate ones being apical, the pistillate basal.

Androphore: A stalk or other supporting structure under stamens raised above their normal position in the flower.

Anemorphilous: With the pollen carried by wind.

Annual: A plant completing its life cycle in a year or less.

Annular: Ring like.

Annular thickening: Thickening of the wall of a xylem cell laid down in the form of a ring.

Annulus: A ring. In the ferns a crest like or other special structure on the sporangium.

Anther: The portion of the stamen which produces pollen.

Anther tube: A tube formed by coalescent anthers, as in the sunflower family.

Antheridium: A structure producing antherozoids, that is male gametes or sex cells.

Antherozoid: A male gamete (sex) cell of a plant.

Anthesis: The time when the flower expands and opens or the process of expansion and opening.

Anthocyanin: Any of a common class of pigments having colours ranging from labender to purple. These pigments are affected by the acidity or alkalinity of the cell sap, and they change colour in approximately the same way as litmus paper, tending towards red in an acid medium and blue in a basic medium. These pigments are water soluble and not associated with plastids.

Antipodal cells: Three cells at the end of the flowering plant megagametophyte opposite the egg.

Antrorse: Directed upward or forward.

Apetalous: Without petals.

Aphyllous: Without leaves.

Apical: Of the apex.

Apical placenta: A placenta at the distal (apical) end of the ovary.

Apiculate: Terminated by an abrupt, short, flexible point.

Apiculation: An abrupt, short, flexible point.

Apocarpous: With the carpels separate.

Apogamous: Developed without the joining of gametes, that is asexually.

Apomixes: In some species the embryo is not produced as a result of meiosis and fertilization, but form a cell in the embryo sac or surrounding nucellus which does not undergo meiosis but develops to form a zygote of same genetic makeup as the female parent.

Apophysis: A swelling on the surface of an organ as, for example, the somewhat swollen exposed portion of the cone scale of a gymnosperm.

Appendiculate: With a basal appendage.

Appressed: Lying tightly against another (Usually larger) organ.

Apterous: Without wings.

Aquatic: Growing in water.

Arachnoid: With slender, tangled hairs resembling the threads of a spider web.

Arboreous: Of tree like form, that is with a main woody trunk.

Arborescent: Of large size and more or less tree like but without the clear distinction of a single trunk.

Archegonium: A flask shaped organ containing an egg, that is, female gamete or sex cell.

Arctic: The area beyond timber line at high latitudes.

Arcuate: Forming a moderate curve or arc.

Areolate: Divided into small, marked-off spaces (Reticulate).

Areole: Diminutive of area; a small, clearly marked space. The term is used most frequently in

reference to the small, special spine-bearing areas on the stem of a cactus.

Aril: A large appendage of the funiculus at the hilum (attachment area) of a seed. It tends to envelope the seed.

Arista: A stiff bristle.

Aristate: with a stiff bristle.

Articulate: with conspicuous segments or joints.

Artificial system: A system made up according to predetermined supposedly important characters.

Ascending: Arising at an oblique angle.

Aseptic: Absence of fungi, bacteria, viruses, mycoplasmas, or other microorganisms in cultures.

Asperous: Rough.

Assurgent: ascending.

Altenuate: With a long, tapering point, this usually set off rather abruptly from the main body of the object (ex. a leaf blade).

Auricle: An appendage shaped like the lobe of a human ear.

Auriculate: Having an artricle.

Austral: Southern.

Autogamy: When a flower is fertilized by its own pollen.

Autonomic: As referred to parthenocarpy, the ability to set fruits without the stimulus resulting from pollination.

Awl-shaped: With a narrow flattened body tapering very gradually upward into a point (subulate).

Awn: A long stout or stiff bristle.

Awned: With an awn.

Axenic: Totally free from association with other organisms.

Axil: The adaxial angle between two organs, particularly the angle between the upper side of a leaf and the stem.

Axile: On the axis, as for example, said of placentae at or near the centre of an ovary.

Axillary: In the axil.

Axillary bud: A bud in a leaf axil.

Axillary flower: A flower in the axil of a leaf or a bract.

Auxin: Auxin is a generic term for compounds characterized by their capacity to induce elongation in shoot cells. They resemble indole-3-acetic acid in physiological action. Auxin may, and generally do, affect other processes besides elongation, but elongation is considered critical. Auxins are generally acids with an unsaturated cyclic nucleus or their derivatives.

Baccate: Berry like, that is, flushy or pulply.

Banner: The upper and usually largest petal in the papilionaceous corolla of a plant of the pea family. Known also as a standard or a vexillum.

Barbed: With a rigid barb like the barb of a fish hook.

Barbellate: Diminutive of barbed (Still smaller, barbellulate).

Barbulate: With a beared of fine hairs.

Bars of sanio: Special thickening on the walls of some xylem cells.

Basal leaves: Leaves at the base of an herbaceous plant arising from several nodes separated by exceedingly short internodes occurring at about ground level.

Basal placenta: A placenta at the basal end of the ovary.

Basifixed: Attached at the base.

Beaked: Ending in a firm elongated slender structure.

Beared: With long or stiff hairs.

Berry: A fleshy or pulpy fruit with more than one seed and formed from either a superior or an inferior ovary. The seeds are embedded in pulpy tissue.

Bidentate: With two teeth.

Biennial: Completing the life cycle in two years. Biennial plants usually produce only basal leaves above the ground the first year and both basal leaves and flowering stems the second.

Bifid: Forked, that is, ending in two parts.

Bilabiate: Two lipped. A bilabiate corolla has petals in two sets commonly with two in the upper and three in the lower.

Bilateral: Two sided.

Bilaterally symmetrical: Capable of division into only two similar sections, which are mirror images of each other.

Bilocular: With two cavities, as an ovary with two seed chambers.

Bipinnate: Pinnate and the primary leaflets again pinnate.

Bipinnatified: Pinnatified with the primary divisions again pinnatified.

Bisexual: With both sexes represented in the same individual or organ *e.g.* with stamens and pistils in the same flower.

Blade: The broad, usually flat part of a leaf.

Bloom: A usually waxy; whitish or bluish powder covering the surface of a leaf, stem, fruit or other organ.

Blossom end: The end of an inferior ovary and the surrounding floral cup which supports the flower parts or at fruiting time the calyx and remains of other flower parts.

Boreal: Northern.

Boss: A protrusion, as for example, a protuberance near the centre of the apophysis of a scale of a gymnosperm cone.

Bract: A leaf subtending a reproductive structure, such as a flower or a cluster of flowers or an ovuliferous scale. Usually the leaf is specialized and at least somewhat dissimilar to the foliage leaves.

Bracteate: With bracts.

Bracteolate: With bractlets.

Bracteole: Diminutive of bract, a mere scale.

Bractlet: A minor bract.

Branchlet: A small branch, that is one of the smallest degree.

Branch primordium: The lump of tissue which develops into a young branch.

Bristle: A stiff hair.

Bryophyta: The mosses, liverworts and anthocerotae.

Bud: A growing structure at the Tip of the stem or a branch, with the enclosing scale leaves or immature leaves; a young flower which has not yet opened. There are vegetative buds and flower buds, as described in the definition above.

Bulb: An underground bud covered by fleshy scales, the coating formed from the bases of leaves.

Bulbiferous: With bulbs.

Bulbils: A small bulb. The word is applied to bulb like structures produced on the stems, usually in the axils of leaves or sometimes in the places where flowers ordinarily occur.

Bulblets: A small underground bulb.

Bulbous: Bulblike.

Bullate: Blistered or puckered.

Caducous: Falling very early. In the poppy family the caduceus sepals fall away when the flower open.

Caespitose: Growing in tufts or mats.

Calcarate: With a spur.

Callosity: A thickened hard structure.

Callous: With the texture of a callus.

Callus: Production of new unspecializing cell from a part of the plant, growing as a result of injury or wounding.

Calyculate: With small bracts in a series below the flower, these resembling a calyx.

Calyptra: A cap, cover or lid.

Calyx: A cup; the sepals of a flower, the outermost series of flower parts. Each sepal has the same number of vascular traces as a leaf of the species. If there is doubt it may be distinguished by this character cf. petal.

Calyx tube: A tube formed from the lower portions of the sepals. The term has been used loosely for (a) a floral cup or floral tube regardless of its origin, (b) a floral cup or tube formed by coalescence and adnation of the bases of the sepals, petals and stamens, (c) a perianth tube of the type in the monocotyledons formed by edge to edge adnation of the adjacent sepals and petals together with the bases of the stamens (d) and the portion of a floral cup or tube above the area of adnation to an inferior ovary.

Cambium: A group of cells which possess the power of active growth and division, and which is responsible for the production of old tissues in matured organs.

Campanulate: Bell shaped, that is, the shape of an inverted church bell *i.e.* rounded at the attachment and with a broad flaring rim.

Campylotropous: Descriptive of an ovule which curves in such a way that the micropyle is near the funiculus or stalk but the side of the ovule is not adnate to the funiculus.

Canaliculated: With lengthwise furrows or channels.

Cancellate: Appearing to be a lattice work.

Canescent: Grayish- white or hoary, densely covered with white or gray fine hairs, these usually short.

Capillary: Like an elongated delicate hair or thread.

Capitate: In a dense cluster or head.

Capitulate: Diminutive of capitate.

Capitulum: A small head.

Caprifig: The wild or 'male' fig, the uncultivated form.

Capsule: A dry, many seeded fruit made up of more than one carpel and splitting open length wise at maturity.

Carina: A keel, literally like the keel of a boat. Sometimes said of a structure which simply is folded and creased and without a projecting keel on the crease.

Carinate: With a keel.

Carpel: A specialized leaf which forms either all or part of a pistil.

Cartilaginous: With the texture of cartilage that is, tough and firm but somewhat flexible.

Caruncle: An appendage at the attachment point of a seed.

Carunculate: With a caruncle.

Caryopsis: The fruit of a grass that is, a one seeded, indehiscent fruit with the pericarp adnate to the seed.

Castaneous: Chestnut coloured.

Catkin: A soft, usually scaly spike or raceme of small apetalous unisexual flowers, the inflorescence usually falling as a single unit.

Caudate: With a talelike structures.

Caudex: A largely underground stem base which persists from year to year and each season produces leaves and flowering stem of short duration.

Caulescent: Having a well developed stem above ground as opposed to having only what appears to be the stalk of the individual flower or cluster of flowers.

Cauline: Of or on the stem.

Cell: The structural and functional unit of living organisms.

Cell culture: This term is used to denote the growing of cells in vitro including the culture of single cells. In cell cultures, the cell are no longer organized into tissues.

Cell hybridization: The fusion of two or more dissimilar cells leading to the formation of a synkaryon.

Cell line: A cell line arises from a primary culture at the time of the first successful subcultures. The term cell line implies that cultures from it consist of numerous lineages of cells originally present in the primary cultures. The terms finite or continuous are used as prefixes if the status of the culture is known. If not, the term line will suffice. The term "continuous line" replaces the term "established line". In any published description of a culture, one must make every attempt to publish the characterization of the history of the culture. If such has already been published, a reference to the original publication must be made. In obtaining a culture from another laboratory, the proper designation of the culture, as originally named and described, must be reported in any publication.

Cell strain: A cell strain is derived either from a primary culture or a cell line by the selection or cloning of cells having specific properties or markers. These properties or markers must persist during subsequent cultivation. In describing a cell strain, its specific features must be defined. The terms finite or continuous are used as prefixes if the status of the culture is known. If not, the term strain will suffice. The term "continuous line" replaces the term "established line". In any published description of a cell strain, one must make every attempt to publish the characterization of the history of the strain. If such has already been published, a reference to the original publication must be made. In obtaining a culture from another laboratory, the proper designation of the culture, as originally named and described must be maintained and any deviations in cultivation from the original should be reported in any publication.

Centrifugal: Developing first at the centre and then gradually toward the outside.

Centripetal: Developing first at the outside and the gradually towards the centre.

Cernuous: Nodding.

Certified seed: Progeny of the registered seed that is produced in the largest volume and sold to the crop producers.

Chaff: Dry, membranous scales or bracts, that is, similar to the chaff which comes from a thrashing machine.

Chaffy: Resembling chaff.

Chamber: A room. Applied to the cavities of an anther or an ovary.

Channeled: With lengthwise grooves, the grooves usually deep.

Chartaceous: Like writing paper.

Chasmogamy: Pollination only after the opening of the flower.

Chimeras: When a mutation occurs within a single cell of a clone it initially produces an "islands" of mutant cells within a growing point of a stem. If successful, the plant then becomes a mixture of two different genotypes. This structural arrangement is known as a chimera.

Chlorophyll: The green colouring of most plants. A substance which aids in making the energy of light available to photosynthesis.

Chloroplast: Literally a green body, actually a solid body with chlorophyll in its outer part.

Chlorosis: A diseased condition shown by loss of green colour.

Choripetalous: With the petals separate or atleast with some of them separate from others.

Cilia: Hairs along the margin of a structure, placed like the eye-lashes on a human eyelid.

Ciliate: With cilia along the margin.

Ciliolate: Diminutive of ciliate.

Cinereous: The colour of ashes.

Circinate: Coiled at the tip, as the young coiled leaf of a fern which uncoils gradually as it develops.

Circumscissile: Opening by a horizontal circular line, the top coming off like a lid.

Class: The next taxon below division; a group of related orders or sometimes a single order.

Clavate: Gradually enlarged upward after the manner of a base-ball bat or the traditional giants club, that is, either tapering gradually upward or with an enlarged knob at the summit.

Clavellate: Diminutive of clavate.

Claw: The narrow stalk at the base of a petal. This resembling the petiole of a leaf.

Cleft: Indented about half way or little more than half way to the base or to the midrib.

Cleistogamy: Self-pollination without the flower opening.

Cleistogamous: Self-fertilized in the bud stage or atleast without opening.

Climbing: Supported by clinging (Scandent).

Clonal propagation: A sexual reproduction of plants that are considered to be genetically uniform and originated from a single individual or explant.

Clone: Genetically uniform material derived from a single individual and propagated exclusively by vegetative means as cuttings, graftage or division.

Coalescence: The union of similar parts as for example, the petals of a flower.

Coalescent: Adjective.

Cochleate: Spiral, like a turban snail.

Coherent: Grown fast together.

Colonial: In colonies. For the angiosperms used, primarily in reference to plants occurring in clumps connected by rhizomes.

Coloure: The failure of blossoms to set, resulting in a pre-matured drop.

Column: A slender aggregation of coalescent stamen. Filaments, as in some members of the mallow family.

Coma: A tuft of hairs on the end of a seed.

Commissure: The surface along which two or more locules are joined to each other.

Comose: With a coma.

Compatible: Ability of pollen to develop in the styles rapidly enough to reach the ovule in time to effect fertilization.

Compatibility: Of sex cells, the ability to unite and form a fertilized egg that can grow to maturity.

Complete flower: A flower with all the four usual series that is sepals, petals stamen and pistils.

Compound: Composed of two or more similar elements.

Compound leaf: It is composed of two or more leaflets, a compound pistil is composed of two or more coalescent carpels.

Compressed: Flattened, particularly from side to side.

Conduplicate: Folded together lengthwise.

Cone: A reproductive structure composed of an axis bearing sporophylls or other seed or pollen bearing structures.

Congeniality: As determined by the degree of success of the union between stock and scion.

Conglomerate: Densely aggregated; a cluster or a heap.

Coniferous: Cone bearing.

Conjugate: Lying together in pairs.

Connate: Joined from the beginning of development.

Connate perfoliate: Both connate and perfoliate.

Connective: The middle part of an anther connecting the two pollen sacs or two pairs of pollen sacs.

Connivent: Standing together. Stamens with their tips ending against each other are connivent.

Contorted: Twisted out of the usual form. Petals may be contorted in the bud.

Convolute: Rolled up lengthwise. Petals may be convolute in the bud.

Cordate: Of a conventional heart-shape, the length greater than the width, the petiole attached in the basal sinus; applied also to the basal indentation of a leaf or other structures.

Coriaceous: Leathery.

Corm: A bulblike structure formed by enargement of the stem base. It is sometimes coated with one or more membranous layers.

Corneous: Horny.

Corolla: The petals of a flower, that is, the inner series (or several series) of the parianth. Each petal has usually a single vascular trace as does a stamen.

Corolla division: A division is longer than a lobe or part.

Corolla lobe: A lobe is longer then the tooth. Lobes may be applied in a broad sense to cover lobes, parts or divisions.

Corolla part: A part is longer than a lobe.

Corolla teeth: The separate tips of the individual petals of a sympetalous corolla.

Corolla tube: The hollow cylinder formed by coalescence of petals.

Corona: A small crown, the term being applied to special appendages of the corolla. These sometimes form a tube.

Coroniform: Shaped like a crown.

Corrugated: With many small folds or wrinkles.

Cortex: The layers of living cells outside the central stele but inside the outermost single layer of cells of a stem or a root.

Cortical: Of the cortex.

Corymb: A flat topped cluster of flowers; fundamentally like a raceme but with the pedicels of the lower flowers longer and the pedicels of the upper flowers gradually shorter.

Corymbiform: In the form of a corymb.

Corymbose: Arranged in corymbs.

Costa: A rib or a promiment nerve.

Costate: Ribbed lengthwise.

Cotyledons: One of the first leaves developed in the embryo in the seed at the joining point of the hypocotyls and the epicotyl. Often food materials are stored in them.

Creeping: The stem growing along the ground and producing adventitious roots.

Crenate: With rounded teeth projecting at right angles to the edge of the leaves.

Crenulate: Diminutive of crenate.

Crested: With a crest, that is a projection at a prominent position such as the apex or the midrib of an organ.

Crinkle: A disorder of apples in which the surface of the fruit becomes roughened. Supposed to be a form of draught injury.

Crisped: Ruffled, that is with the same bind of winding as in sinuate, but in the vertical plane instead of the horizontal.

Cristate: Crested.

Cristulate: The diminutive of cristate.

Cross-pollination: Transfer of pollen grain from a flower of one variety to a flower of another variety.

Cross-compatible: The pollen of one variety 'A' is capable of functioning in the styles and fertilizing the ovules of variety 'B' (variety 'B', however, may not be cross-compatible with 'A').

Cross-incompatible: Variety 'A' produces functional sex cells, but its pollen tube grows too slowly in the styles of variety 'B' to effect fertilization. Variety 'A' may, however, serve as an effective pollinizer for some other varieties. (Variety 'B' mar serve as an effective pollinizer for variety 'A').

Cross-fertile: One variety 'A' is used as a pollinizer for another variety 'B' and 'B' produces fruit with viable seed.

Cross-fruitful: One variety 'A' is used as a pollinizer for another variety 'B' and 'B' produces a commercial crop.

Cross-pollination: The transfer of pollen from the anthers of a flower of one variety to the stigma of a flower of a different variety.

Cross-unfruitful: One variety 'A' is used as a pollinizer for another variety 'B', and 'B' fails to produce a commercial crop.

Cross-sterile: One variety 'A' is used as a pollinizer for another variety 'B', and 'B' fails to produce fruit with viable seed.

Cross section: A slice cut across an object.

Cruciate, cruciform: Cross like.

Crustaceous: Hard and brittle in texture.

Cryptogames: An old term applied to the thallophytes, bryophytes and the pteridophytes, that is the plants which regularly reproduce with out formation of seeds.

Cucullate: Hood shaped

Culum: The hallow stem of a grass, the term being applied some times to ridges also.

Cuneate, cuneiform: Wedge shaped; essentially a narrow isosceles triangle with the distal corners rounded off. The petiole of a cuneate leaf is attached at the sharp angle.

Cupule: A little cup.

Cuspidate: With a sharp, firm point at the tip, as applied to leaves, the term indicates a point of firmer texture than the rest of the blade.

Cuticle: The waxy, more or less waterproof coating secreted by the cells of the epidermis of a leaf, stem or flower parts.

Cyathiform: Cup shaped.

Cyathium: A cuplike involucre enclosing flowers.

Cycle: A circle. Leaves or flower parts arranged in a single series at a single node or in a cycle.

Cyclic: Arranged in a cycle.

Cylindroidal: In approximately the shape of a cylinder.

Cyme: A broad, more or less flat-topped cluster of flowers.

Cymose: With cyme like cluster of flowers.

Cymule: Diminutive of cyme.

Cypsela: An achene which is attached to the enclosing floral cup or tube, that is, an achene formed from an inferior ovary.

Cytology: The study of cell. Often particular emphasis is placed upon the chromosomes.

Cytoplasm: The living substance outside the nucleus and inside the enclosing membrane.

Deciduous: Falling off at the end of each growing season.

Deciduous tree: Tree which shed their leaves during winter months to enable them to stand cold injury.

Declinate: Bending or curving downward or forward.

Declined: Bending over in one direction.

Decompound: More than one compound.

Decombent: Reclining except at the apex.

Decurrent: Leaf bases which continue along the stem as wings or lines.

Decussate: In opposite pairs with the alternate pairs projecting at right angles to each other.

Deflexed: Abruptly bent or turned downward.

Defined medium: A nutritive solution for culturing cells in which each component is of known chemical structure. Although it is recognized that even the "Purest" chemical compounds may have some contaminants, high quality chemicals should be used with analytic data, if possible, on contaminants.

Dehisce: The split open along definite lines.

Dehiscence: The process of splitting open at maturity.

Dehiscent: Splitting open along definite lines.

Deltoid: Of the shape of the greek letter delta, that is, an equilateral triangle, the attachment being in the middle of one side.

Dentate: With angular teeth projecting at right angles to the edge of the structure.

Denticulate: Diminutive of dentate.

Depauperate: Stunted, that is, very small.

Depressed: Flattened from above as if pushed downward.

Determinate: With a definite predetermined number of structures.

Diadelphous: In two brotherhoods, the term being applied to stamens coalescent in two sets.

Diandrous: With two stamens.

Dichasium: A cyme with two axis running in opposite directions, that is, the type of cyme formed in plants with opposite branching in the inflorescence. See cyme.

Dichlamydeous: With both calyx and corolla.

Dichogamy: Insuring cross-pollination by the sexes being developed at different times.

Dichotomous: Forking, with two usually equal branches at each point of forking.

Dicotyledonous: With two cotyledons.

Dicliny: Male and female organ separate and in different flowers.

Didymous: Twin like, that is, occurring in pairs.

Didynamous: In two pairs, the pairs not being of the same length. The term is applied to stamen.

Diffuse: Spreading widely and diffusely in all directions.

Digitate: Resembling the fingers of a human hand, that is, with several similar structures arising at a common point. See palmate.

Digynous: With two pistils.

Dimerous: With two members; the flower parts in two.

Dimidiate: With the appearance of being only half a structure.

Dimorphous: With two forms.

Dioecious: Unisexual, the male and female elements in different individuals.

Diploid: With 2n chromosomes per cell.

Diplostemonous: The stamens in two series, those of outer series alternating with the petals.

Dipterous: With two wings.

Disc, disk: In the compositae, the central portion of the compound receptacle bearing the disc flowers.

Disc flowers: One of the flowers with tubular corollas.

Disciform: Circular and flattened like disc.

Discoid: Resembling a disc.

Discrete: Separate.

Dissected: Divided into narrow segments.

Dissepiment: A portion dividing an ovary or a fruit into chambers.

Distichous: In two vertical series.

Distinct: Separate.

Diurnal: Occuring in the day time. The term is applied to the flowers which open in day light as opposed to the nocturnal flowers which open at night.

Divaricate: Spreading widely, that is, divergent.

Divergent: Spreading away from each other.

Divided: Indented essentially to the base or midrib.

Division: The highest rank of taxon in the plant kingdom, a group of related classes or some times a single class; a segment of a structure, such as leaf.

Dormant: Applied to buds when they are not actively growing and to plants when they are not in leaf.

Dorsal: On the outer surface of an organ, that is, the side away from the axis.

Dorsiventral: A structure having a clear differentiation of a back and front or upper and lower side.

Dorsoventral: The distance or measurement from the back of a structure to the front, that is, from dorsal to ventral, as opposed to lateral distance.

Double samara: A Samara with two locules and two wings.

Downy: Finely and softly pubescent.

Drainage area: The watershed or area into which the excess precipitation of a region drains.

Drupaceous: Druplike.

Drupe: A fruit with a fleshy exocarp and a hard, stony endocarp about each seed. The term is used also for other fruits which are fleshy or pulpy on the outside and with one or more stones inside.

Drupelet: Diminutive of drupe. The cluster of fruits of a blackberry or raspberry is composed of druplets which seem to form a single fruit.

Echinate: covered with prickles.

Egg: A female gamete cell of a plant.

Effective bloom: The length of time the tree is in conspicuous blossom.

Ellipsoid, ellipsoidal: Elliptical in outline with three-dimensional body.

Elliptic, elliptical: In the form of an ellipse, that is, about one and one half times as long as broad, widest at the middle and rounded at both ends. A two dimensional figure.

Emarginate: With a shallow broad notch at the apex.

Embryo: The new plant enclosed in the seed. Its formation follows union of gametes.

Embryo culture: In vitro development or maintenance of isolated mature or immature embryos.

Embryogenesis: The process of embryo initiation and development.

Embryo sac: The cell in the ovule in which the embryo is formed.

Emersed: Above water.

Enation: An outgrowth from the superficial tisssues of the stem.

Endimic: Restricted in occurrence to aparticular geographical area.

Endocarp: The inner layer of the wall of a fruitified ovary.

Endosperm: A cell layer occurring in at least the immature seeds of flowering plants.

Ensiform: Sword like; in the form of sword.

Entire: without division or toothing of any bind.

Entomophilous: Insect pollinated.

Emphemeral: Lasting for a brief period.

Epicotyl: The portion of the embryo of a seed plant just above the cotyledons, the young stem.

Epigynous: The sepals, petals and stamens apparently upon the ovary, but actually growing from the edge of the floral cup, which is adnate to the ovary.

Epigynous disc: A disc within the floral cup and on top of the inferior ovary.

Epiphyte: A plant growing upon another plant but not parasitic upon it.

Equitant: With the leaves folded around a stem after the manner of the legs of a rider around a horse or some times with the leaves folded around each other in rows.

Errect: Standing upright.

Erose: With the margin appearing to have been gnawes.

Etiolated: White through failure to develop chlorophyll.

Euploid: The situation which exists when the nucleus of a cell contains exact multiples of the haploid number of chromosomes.

Even pinnate: Without a terminal leaflet.

Exocarp: The outer layer of the wall of a fruitified ovary.

Excentric: Off centre.

Excortis: A shelling off the bark of tree.

Excurrent: Projecting as for example, a leaf base which projects beyond the margin of the blade.

Exfoliating: Separating into thin layer.

Exocarp: The outer layer of the pericarp.

Explant: Tissue taken from its original site and transferred to an artifical medium for growth and maintenance.

Explanate: Flattened and spread out.

Exserted: Projecting beyond the usual containing structure.

Extraterritorial: Occuring beyond the specific geographical range of some features of this book *i.e.* beyond the north America north of Mexico.

Extrose: Facing outward.

Falcate: In the shape of a scythe, that is curving, flat and tapering gradually to a point.

False partition: An ovary partition not formed by infolding of the edges of the carpel, growing from the middle of the placenta on the opposite side or formed by ingrowth of placentae.

Farinose: Mealy, that is composed of mealy granules or with granules on the surface.

Fasciate: Literally, in a bundle or bundled together, the term being applied as fascinated, to branches remaining parallel and grown abnormally together.

Fasciation: A deformity in which the stem becomes much flattened as a result of multiple terminal buds arranged in a single plane.

Fascicle: A bundle or cluster.

Fastigiate: Errect and close together.

Faveolate or favose: Resembling a honey comb.

Fecundation: The fusions of two gametes to form a new cell.

Fecundity: The ability of flowers to produce seeds that will germinate.

Female gamete: An egg; a female gamete cell.

Fenestrate: Perforated.

Ferruginous: Rust coloured.

Fertile: Productive, mean capable of producing fruit or spores. Sometimes a staminate flower is referred to as infertile or sterile because it produces no seed.

Fertility: The ability to set and mature fruit with viable seed.

Fertilization: The union of male germ cell, contained in the pollen grain, with the female germ cell, or egg, in the ovule.

Fibrillose: With fine fibres.

Fibrous root system: A root system with several major roots about equal and arising from approximately the same point.

Field capacity: Is defined as the amount of water held against the force of gravity.

Filament: A thread; the stalk of a stamen.

Filamentous: Composed of threads.

Filiform: Thread like, that is, long slender and cylindroidal.

Fimbriate: Fringed, that is resembling the fring on the sleeve of an early American buckskin shirt.

Fimbrillate: The diminutive of fimbriate.

Fimbriolate: With a very fine fringe.

Fistulose: Hollow and cylindroidal.

Flabellate: Fan shaped.

Flaccid: Weak.

Flagelliform: Whiplike or lash like.

Flates: They are shallow plastic, styrofoam, wooden or metal trays with drainage holes in the bottom. They are useful for germinating seeds or rooting cuttings, since they permit young plants to be moved easily.

Fleshy fruits: A fruit with soft, juicy tissues.

Flexuous: Curved in first one direction, then the opposite.

Floccose: With tufts of wooly hair.

Flocculent: Diminutive of floccose.

Floral cup: A cup bearing on its rim the sepals, petals and stamens; originating as (a) a hypanthium. (b) a "calyx tube" formed by coalescence and adnation of the bases of the sepals, petals and stamens, or (c) a perianth tube of the type in the monocotyledons, the sepals and adjacent petals being adnate edge to edge.

Floral tube: An elongated, slender floral cup.

Floret: A small flower, the flower of a grass and the two immediately enclosing bracts, that is the lemma and palea.

Floricana: A canelike stem producing flowers.

Floriferous: Bearing flowers.

Flower: A complex strobilus formed at the end of a branch, including the receptacle (thalamus or torus) and bearing sepals, stamens, petals and pistils or some of these.

Flower bud: A bud which will develop into a flower, actually the young flower.

Flowering hormones: Are hormones which initiate the formation of floral primodia, or promote their development.

Flowering regulators: Are regulators which affect flowering.

Foliaceous: Leaflike.

Foliage bud: A bud containing new young leaves.

Foliage leaf: The green leaf of the mature plant.

Foliar: Relating to a leaf.

Foliate: Leaved, an example being 3- foliate or trifoliate.

Foliolate: With leaflets.

Foliose: Bearing many leaves.

Follicle: A dry fruit formed from a single carpel, containing more than one seed, and splitting open along the suture. The term is applied also sometimes to similar fruits splitting only along the midrib.

Follicular: Of the nature of a follicle.

Forked: Dividing into branches which are nearly equal.

Foundation seeds: Progeny of breeders seed which is so handled as to maintain the highest standard of genetic identity and purity.

Foveolate: Pitted.

Free: Separate from other organs (distinct).

Friability: A term indicating the tendency for plant cells to separate from one another.

Frond: The leaf blade of a fern.

Frondose: Leafy, that is with frond like leaves.

Fruit: A matured ovary with its enclosed seeds and some times with attached external structures.

Fruitescent: Shrubby or becoming so at length.

Fruitful: A plant or variety that sets and matures a commercial crop of fruit.

Fruiticose: Distinctly woody, living over from year to year, and attaining considerable size, with several main stems instead of a single trunk.

Fruit setting: A development of the ovary and adjacent tissues following the blossoming period.

Fugacious: Falling away early.

Fulbous: Tawny.

Fungus: A plant without chlorophyll and with no vascular tissue, stems or leaves. Plural fungi.

Funiculus: The stalk of an ovule or a seed.

Funnelform: In the shape of a funnel.

Furcate: Forked.

Fusicous: Grayish-brown.

Fusiform: In the shape of a spindle, that is, widest at the middle and tapering gradually to each pointed end, the body being circular in cross section.

Galea: A hood formed from a portion of the parianth derived, for example, from the two upper petals coalascent indistinguishably into one or from the upper sepal.

Galeate: With a galea.

Gamete: A unisexual cell which must fuse with another gamete to produce a new individual.

Gamopetalous: With all the petals coalescent (Sympetalus).

Gametophyte: The gamete producing generation, each cell with a chromosomes.

Geminiate: Equal or arranged in pairs.

Generative cell: A cell in the microgametophyte (or pollen grain) which may give rise directly or indirectly to male gamete cells or nuclei.

Genetics: The study of heredity.

Geniculate: Bent like the human knee.

Genus: A group of related species or sometimes a single species. Plural, genera.

Gibbous: Swollen or distended on one side.

Glabrate: At first hairy but latter becoming glabrous.

Glabrous: not hairy.

Gladiate: Sword like.

Gland: A secreting organ.

Glandular: Bearing glands, small cellular organs secreting oils, tars, resins *etc.* often only the secretion is visible.

Glaucescent: More or less glaucous.

Glaucous: Covered with a white or bluish powder or bloom, this often composed of finely divided particles of wax. Ex. The bloom on a plum.

Globose, globular: Spheroidal.

Glochid: A sharp hair or bristle tipped with a barb.

Glochidiate: Barbed at the tip.

Glomerate: In compact clusters.

Glomerulate: Diminutive of glumerate.

Glomerule: A single cyme of sessile flowers forming a compact cluster. It may be distinguished from a head by blooming of the central flower first.

Glumaceous: Resembling a glume of a grass spikelet.

Glume: One of the two chaff like bractlets at the base of a grass spikelet. The glumes do not enclose flowers.

Glutinous: covered with sticky material.

Granulose: Covered by minute grains of hardened material.

Gregarious: In large colonies.

Growth hormones: A hormone which regulate growth.

Growth regulators: (Synonym: growth sunstances) are regulators which affect growth.

Gummosis: A disorder particularly of stone and citrus fruit, in which there are copious exudations or deposites of gum.

Gum spots: A disorder of stone, citrus and certain other fruits in which there are small local deposites of gum in the tissues of fruits, shoot or other organ.

Gymnospermous: With the seeds naked, that is not enclosed in an ovary.

Gynandrium: A structure formed by adnation of stamens and pistil.

Gynandrous: With the stamen adhering to the pistils.

Gynecandrous: With staminate and pistillate flowers in the same inflorescence, the pistillate above and the staminate below.

Gynobase: An enlarged or elongated portion of the receptacle bearing the pistil.

Gynoecium: The pistil of a flower or its group of pistils.

Gynophore: A special stalk under a pistil.

Habit: The general appearance of a plant.

Habitate: The type of locality or the set of ecological conditions under which the plant grows.

Hair: A slender cellular projection.

Halberd-shaped: Hastate.

Halophyte: A plant growing in salty soil as for example an alkali flat or a salt water marsh.

Hamate: With a hook at the tip.

Haploid: With a chromosomes per cell.

Hastate: More or less sagittate (arrow head shaped) but with the divergent basal lobes.

Head: A cluster of sessile or essentially sessile flowers or fruits at the apex of a peduncle. Essentially a spike with a very short axis.

Helicoid: Spiral, like the shell of a turban snail.

Helicoid cyme: A coiled inflorescence. The main stem terminates in a flower and a single bud just below grows out as a stem but terminates also in a flower, the process being repeated many times and always in the same direction.

Herb: A non woody plant, at laeast one which is not woody above ground level.

Herbaceous: Not woody.

Herbarium: A collection of pressed plant specimens.

Hermaphrodite: Bisexual, that is, with stamens and pistils in the same flower.

Heterocarpous: Producing more than one kind of fruit.

Heterogamous: With more than one kind of flower.

Heterogeneous: Of various binds, that is, not all individuals the same.

Heteroploid: The term given to a cell culture when the cells comprising the culture possess nuclei containing chromosome numbers other than the diploid number. This ia a term used only to describe a culture and is not used to describe the individual cells. Thus, a heteroploid culture would be one which contains aneuploid cells.

Hilium: The point of attachment of the funiculus (Stalk) to the seed.

Hip (of a rose): A floral cup which usually becomes enlarged and fleshy at fruiting time. The true fruits are achenes inside.

Hippocrepiform: Horse shoe shaped.

Hirsute: With fairly coarse more or less stiff hairs.

Hirsutulus: Slight hirsute.

Hispid: With rigid or stiff bristles or bristly hairs.

Hispidulous: Diminutive of hispid.

Hoary: Covered with short, dense, grayish white hairs, the surface of the stem, leaf or other structure therefore appearing white.

Homogamous: With only one kind of flower.

Homogeneous: With all members similar.

Hood: A hoodlike structure, often formed from a petal or a sepal or more than one of either.

Humifuse: Spreading on the ground.

Hyaline: Thin and membranous being transparent or translucent.

Hybrid: Produced by dissimilar parents.

Hydrophyte: An aquatic plant.

Hygroscopic: Changing form with changes of moisture content.

Hygroscopic coefficient: The percentage of soil water retained in contact with a saturated atmosphere and in the absence of any other source of moisture.

Hypanthium: A floral cup or tube developed by extra growth of the margin of the receptacle. An alternative adopted by some authors in use of hypanthium with the meaning of floral cup.

Hypocotyl: The portion of the axis of an embryo of a seed plant just below the cotyledon(s).

Hypogaeous: Below the ovary, that is, referring to flower parts which come directly from the receptacle and not from a floral cup or tube. A hypogynous flower is one which does not have a floral cup or tube.

Hypogynous disc: A flushy cushion of tissue growing from the receptacle below the ovary, often the stamens and sometimes the petals being attached to it.

Imbricate: overlapping like the shingles on a roof.

Imparipinnate: Odd pinnate.

Implexed: Tangled, interlacing.

Implicate: Woven in.

Inactive bud: A bud dormant either before the beginning of the growing season or through a longer period.

Incanous: Covered with white hairs.

Included: Not protruding beyond the normal surrounding structures.

Incompatible: Inability of viable pollen to develop in the styles rapidly enough to reach the ovule in time to effect fertilization.

Incompatibility: Of sex cells, the inability to unite and form a fertilized egg that can be grown to maturity.

Incomplete flower: A flower lacking one or more of the four usual series of structures, that is, sepals, petals, stamens or pistils.

Incrassate: Thickened.

Incumbent: Applied to a pair of cotyledons which lie with the back of one against the axis of the embryo.

Indehiscent: Not opening by splitting along regular lines or not opening at all.

Indeterminate: Of indefinite growth *i.e.* the size or number of organs to be produced not predetermined.

Indigenous: Native in a particular region.

Indument: A covering of hairs.

Induplicate: With the edges folded inward.

Indurate: Hardened.

Indusium: The membranous covering of a sorus of a pteridophyte.

Inferior: Below.

Inferior floral cup: The portion of a floral cup or tube adnate to the wall of an inferior ovary.

Infertile: Varieties 'A' and 'B' both produce fruit with viable when pollinated by each other.

Inflorescence: The flowering area or segment of a plant.

Integument: The outer coating of an ovule, a structure grown up from the sporophyll and surrounding the sporangium. The integument becomes the seedcoat.

Intercompatible: The pollen produced by either variety of a combination is capable of functioning in the styles and fertilizing the ovule of the other variety.

Interfruitful: Varieties 'A' and 'B' both produce commercial crops when pollinated by each other.

Interincompatible: Varieties 'A' and 'B' are unfruitful when pollinated by each other because the pollen tubes of each variety grow too slowly in the styles of the other to effect fertilization. Either variety may serve as an effective pollinizer for some other varieties.

Intersterile: Varieties 'A' and 'B' both fail to produce fruit with viable seed when pollinated by each other.

Interstock: It is a piece of stem inserted by means of two graft unions between the scion and the rootstock.

In vitro propagation: Propagation of plants in controlled, artificial environment, using plastic or glass cultures vessels, aseptic techniques, and a defined growing medium.

In vitro transformation: A heritable change, occurring in cells in culture, either intrinsically or from treatment with chemical carcinogens, oncogenic viruses, irradiation, *etc.*, and leading to the acquisition of altered morphological, antigenic, neoplastic, proliferative, or other properties.

Involucel: The involucre of a secondary umbel.

Involucre: A series of bracts surrounding a flower cluster or some times a single flower.

Irregular: Used in botany to indicate a bilaterally symmetrical structure as for example, a

bilaterally symmetrical flower.

Isomerous: With the members of the various series of flower parts of equal number.

Keel: A ridge along the outside of a fold, like the keel of a boat. The term is applied to the two coalescent lower petals of a papilionaceous corolla of the pea family.

Labiate: With lips, that is, two opposed structures as for example, the upper two petals as opposed to lower three petals in the mint family.

Lanolin: The natural fat of wool.

Latent bud: A bud, usually concealed, more than one year old, which may remain dormant indefinitely or may develop under certain conditions.

Lateral bud: One in a leaf axil.

Legume: A dry several seeded fruit formed from a single carpel and dehiscent on both margins.

Locular: Divided into locules.

Loculicidal: Dehiscent along the midrib of a carpel of an ovary containing more than one carpel and chamber.

Lodicule: One of the two small scales at the base of the grass flower.

Loment: A legume divided by constriction into a linear series of segments each containing one seed.

Male gamete: An antherozoid or a male gamete cell or nucleus.

Male nucleous: The male gamete of a flowering plant, that is, a single nucleus with the associated cytoplasm but with no cell wall.

Megagametophyte: A female gametophyte.

Megasporangium: A sporangium producing megaspore.

Megaspore: A larger type of spore developed by a plant with spores of two sizes or kinds.

Megasporophyll: A sporophyll bearing one or more megasporangia.

Mericarp: A portion of a fruit which appears to be a whole fruit.

Mericloning: A popular term, not in scientific usage, referring to the in vitro vegetative propagation of orchids from excised shoot tips, axillary buds, or floral organs.

Meristem: A plant tissue in which the cells are capable of, under favourable growth conditions usually in process of active division, to produce new daughter cells.

Meristem culture: In vitro culture of a generally shiny dome-like structure measuring less than 0.1 mm in length when excised, most often excised from the shoot apex.

Meristemming: A popular term, not in scientific usage, referring to the in vitro clonal propagation of plants from various explant sources including shoot tips, leaf section and calli; shoot apical meristems are seldom used.

Meristemoid: Meristem-like cells located in areas of a plant or culture other than the meristem.

Mesocarp: The middle layer of a pericarp.

Metaxenia: The supposed direct influence of the pollen or pollen parent on the characteristics of the developing fruit.

Micropropagation: This term is synonymous with in vitro propagation.

Morphogenesis: The process of growth and development of differentiated structures.

Microspore: The smaller type of spore in a plant producing spores of two sizes.

Mixed bud: A bud containing both leaf primordial and rudimentary flowers.

Monoadelphous: In one botherhood; referring to stamens with their filaments coalescent into a single tube.

Monochlamydeous: With a single series in the perianth that is only the sepals.

Monoecious: The stamens and pistils in separate flowers borne on the same individual.

Naked bud: A bud not covered by special scales but only by the outer leaves.

Nocturnal: Occuring at night. The term is applied to flowers which open at night.

Nucellus: The sporangium enclosed in the ovule of a seed plant.

Nut: A hard, relatively large, indehiscent, 1 seeded fruit.

Nutlet: Diminutive of nut.

Nutrients: Are defined as materials which supply either energy or essential mineral elements.

Order: A tascon composed of related families or sometimes of a single family.

Organ culture: The maintenance or growth of organ primordial or the whole or parts of an organ in vitro in a way that may allow differentiation and preservation of the architecture and/or function.

Organogenesis: The evolution, from dissociated cells, of a structure which shows natural organ

form or function or both.

Osmosis: The passage of water through a semi-permeable membrane.

Ovary: In the flower, that portion of the female organ which contains the potential seeds (ovules). After fertilization it grows into the fruit.

Ovulate: Producing ovules.

Ovules: The potential seed before fertilization.

Panicle: A cluster of associated spikes racemes or corymbs.

Papilionaceous: Butterfly like.

Pappus: The specialized calyx of members of the sunflower family; composed of bristles or scales.

Parthenocarpy: The development of edible fruit without fertilization. Parthenocarpic fruits are seedless.

Parthenogenetic: Developing without fertilization

Partly inferior ovary: With only the basal portion of the ovary adnate to the floral cup.

Passage: The transfer or transplantation of cells, with or without dilution, from one culture vessel to another. It is understood that any time cells are transferred from one vessel to another, a certain portion of he cells may be lost and, therefore, dilution of cells, whether deliberate or not, may occur. This term is synonymous with the term "subculture".

Passage number: The number of times the cells in the culture have been subcultured or passaged. In descriptions of this process, the ratio or dilution of the cells should be stated so that the relative cultural "age" can be ascertained.

Peat: It consists of remains of a aquatic, marsh, bog or swamp vegetation which has been preserved under water in a partially decompose state.

Pectinate: Resembling a comb.

Pedicel: The internode below a flower.

Peduncle: The stalk of a cluster of flowers or the next to the last internode below a single flower.

Pentagynous: With five pistils.

Pentandrous: With five stamens.

Pepo: A fruit of the type in the gourd family, that is, with a hard or leathery rind on the outside and fleshy placental tissue inside. The seeds are numerous and there is only one chamber.

Perfect: A flower having both functional pistils and functional stamens.

Perennation: A lasting state referring particularly to the persistence of fruit long after its usual season of maturity.

Perianth: A collective term for the calyx and the corolla.

Perianth tube: A tube formed by coalescence and adnation of the lower portions of the sepals and petals.

Pericarp: The wall of a matured ovary, that is, the wall of the fruit or the inner wall if the ovary is inferior.

Perigynium: A special sac which encloses the ovary of calyx.

Perigynous: Descriptive of the parts of a flower attached to a floral cup or tube which is not adnate to the ovary. A perigynous flower has a floral cup but the ovary is not adnate to it.

Perigynous disc: A disc adnate to the floral cup of a perigynous flower.

Perlite: It is a graywhite silicaceous material of volcanic origin, mined from larva flows.

Permanent wilting point: The amount of water in soils when rapidly growing plants fail to recover from wilting under condition of low transpiration.

Petal: One member of the series of flower parts forming the corolla.

Petaloid: Resembling a petal in colour and texture.

Photosynthesis: The process of combining in the presence of chlorophyll and light of carbon dioxide and water yielding glucose and oxygen.

Photosynthetic: Descriptive of a green portion of a plant capable of carrying on photosynthesis.

Pistil: The female organ of a flower.

Pistillate: Having pistils, that is, a flower which has pistils but no stamens.

Placenta: The tissue of an ovary which bears ovules or seeds.

(Plant) Hormones: (Synonym: phytohormones) are regulators produced by plants, which in low concentrations regulate plant physiological processes. Hormones usually move within the plants from a site of production to a site of action.

(Plant) Regulators: Are organic compounds, other than nutrients which in small amount promote, inhibit or otherwise modify any physiological process in plants.

Plating efficiency: The percentage of cells plated which give rise to colonies. The total number of cells in the inoculum, type of culture vessel and the environment conditions (medium, temperature, closed or open system, *etc.*) must always be stated. This term is often expressed as the percentage of individual cells in the vessel which give rise to colonies. If one is certain that each of the colonies arose from single cells, then one may properly apply the term "cloning efficiency".

Pollen: The spheroidal structures produced in an anther of a flower or in the microsporophyll of a gymnosperm. The pollen grains are microgametophytes developed from microspores.

Pollen sac: Pollen bearing cavity.

Pollen tube: A tube developed by a pollengrain and growing through the microphyle of an ovule

where its contained cells or nuclei effect fertilization of the egg.

Pollination: The transfer of pollen to the stigma; or in a broad sense, the distribution of pollen. Pollination may be accomplished by insects, wind, gravity, water, birds and artificial methods derived by man.

Pollinizer: The variety (plant) used to furnish pollen. The male parent.

Polyadelphous: In several brotherhoods; with several groups of coalescent stamens.

Polyandrous: With an indefinite large number of stamens.

Polyembryony: Production of more than one embryo in a single ovule.

Polygamo-dioecious: With hermaphrodite and unisexual flowers on different individuals of the same species.

Polygamo-monoecious: Polygamous but in the main monoecious.

Polygamous: With bisexual and unisexual flowers on the same or different individuals of the species.

Polygynous: With a large indefinite number of pistils.

Polymorphic: With several or many forms.

Polyploid: With several to many times n chromosomes per cell.

Population density: The number of cells per unit area or volume of a culture vessel. Also, the number of cells per unit volume of medium in a suspension culture.

Pome: A fleshy fruit with several seed chambers, this formed from an inferior ovary, the fleshy tissue being largely the floral cup, the seeds not embedded in pulp. Apples and pears are the classical examples.

Prickle: A sharp, pointed outgrowth from the superficial tissues of the stem, that is, from the epidermis or the cortex, as in a rose prickle. The structure is not associated with the conducting tissues at the centre of the stem.

Primary culture: A culture started from cells, tissues or organs taken directly from organisms. A primary culture may be regarded as such until it is successfully subcultured for the first time. It then becomes "cell line".

Protandry: The pollen being discharged before the pistils are receptive.

Protogyny: The pistils being receptive before the anthers have ripe pollen.

Pruinose: Covered with a bloom, that is, finely divided particles of a waxy powder.

Protoplast: A plant cell without its outer retaining cell wall.

Protoplast fusion: Technique in which protoplasts are fused into a single cell.

Pruning: Means removing certain parts of the tree in order to modify and utilize its natural habits so that more and better fruit can be obtained at less cost over a longer period.

Pumice: Increases aeration and drainage in a propagation mix and can be used alone or mixed with peat moss.

Raceme: An inflorescence composed of pedicelled flowers arranged along an axis which elongates for an indefinite period. The lower flower blooms first and eventually the terminal bud forms the last flower.

Racemiform: In the form of a raceme.

Rachis: The axis of a pinnate leaf or of an inflorescence.

Ray: A pedicel within an umbel; a ray flower or its corolla.

Ray flower: In the sunflower family, one of the flowers with a ligulate corolla. The flattening is due to failure of complete coalescence between two petals of the sympetalous corolla.

Receptacle: The apical area beyond the pedicle, that is, the portion which bears flower parts. The receptacle consists of several or many nodes and short internodes.

Regular: Radially symmetrical.

Reproductive bud: A bud developing into a flower, cone or other pollen-, seed- or spore bearing structures.

Resting bud: An inactive bud.

Rockwool: This material is used as a rooting and growing medium.

Rouging: The removal of off-type plants or plants of other varieties.

Rosette: A condition in which the internodes are much shortened giving the leaves a bunched or clustered appearance.

Salverform: Descriptive of a sympetalous corolla with the slender basal tube abruptly expanded into a flat or saucer shaped upper portion.

Samara: A dry indehiscent fruit with a wing.

Sand: It consists of small rock particles 0.05-2.0 mm in diameter, formed as a result of weathering of various rocks, its mineral composition depending upon the type of rock.

Scape: A flowering stem which bears no leaves or only a small bract or a pair or whorl of bracts.

Schizocarp: A fruit which splits into one seeded sections (mericarp).

Scion: It is the short piece of detached, shoot containing several dormant buds which, when united with rootstock, comprises the upper portion of graft.

Scorpioid: Often used as descriptive of an inflorescence which is coiled in the bud stage as in the forget me not or fiddle neck. This is a helicoids cyme although it appears to be a spike or a raceme.

Seed: A mature ovule consisting of an integument (seed coat), an enclosed nucellus, the remains of the megagametophyte, the endosperm and embryo.

Seed coat: The outer coating of a seed developed from the integument of the ovule.

Seed dormancy: It is a condition where seeds will not germinate even when the environmental conditions (water, temperature and aeration) are permissive for germination. This not only prevents immediate germination but also regulates the time, conditions and place that germination will occur.

Self-fertile: The ability of a variety to produce fruit with viable seed following self-pollination.

Self-pollination: The transfer of pollen from the anthers of a flower to one variety to the stigma of a flower of the same variety.

Self-sterile: The inability of a variety to produce fruit with viable seed following self-pollination. (Some varieties may be self-fruitful, even though they are self-sterile, because of their ability to produce parthenocarpic fruits.).

Self-unfruitful: A variety which is unable to set and mature a commercial crop of fruit with its own pollen (or as a result of parthenocarpic fruit development).

Sepal: One of the flower parts of the outer series, the sepal forming a calyx.

Septicidal: Descriptive of a fruit dehiscent through the partitious between the seed chambers.

Silique: The elongate capsular fruit of the mustard family which has two seed chambers separated by a false partition from the middle of one placenta to the middle of other. The false partition in this case results from presence of some fertile and some sterile carpels in the pistil.

Sod culture: A method of orchard soil management in which a permanent perennial crop is grown between the trees. Mowed once or twice during growing season and then allowed to remain on the ground. A limited area around the tree is hoed, spaded or otherwise tilled.

Sod mulch: A method of charged soil management in which a permanent perennial crop is grown between the trees, mowed once or twice during the growing season and then allowed to remain on the ground.

Somaclonal variation: This type of genetic variation occurs when plant cells of certain species were grown in culture and new plant regenerated.

Somatic cell hybrid: The cell or plant resulting from the fusion of animal cells or plant protoplasts, respectively, derived from somatic cells which genetically.

Somatic hybridization: The in vitro fusion of animal cells or plant protoplasts derived from somatic cells which differ genetically.

Spadix: A spike with a fleshy or succulent axis, the flowers often partly embedded in the axis.

Spathe: A large bract enclosing an inflorescence at least when it is young. Spathes are either white or highly coloured but usually not green.

Species: A group of related varieties or often a single unit.

Spike: An inflorescence in which the sessile flowers are arranged along an axis. The basal flower blooms first, the last one formed is at the apex.

Spur: An elongated sac produced from a part of a flower as in the larkspur from a sepal or in the columbines from a petal.

Stage I: A step in vitro propagation characterized by the establishment of an asceptic tissue culture of a plant.

Stage II: A step in vitro propagation characterized by the rapid numerical increase of organs or other structures.

Stage III: A step in vitro propagation characterized by the preparation of propagule for successful transfer to soil, a process involving rooting of shoot cuttings, hardening of plants and initiating the change from the heterotrophic to the autotrophic state.

Stage IV: A step in vitro propagation characterized by the establishment in soil of a tissue culture derived plant, either after undergoing a Stage II pretransplant treatment or, in certain species, after the direct transfer of plants from Stage II into soil.

Stamen: The pollen-producing structure of a flowering plant, consisting of an anther and of a filament.

Staminodium: A sterile stamen, that is, without an anther or at least not producing pollen.

Stem end: The basal portion of an inferior ovary at fruiting time, the point of attachment of the pedicel.

Stigma: The apical portion of a pistil *i.e.* the portion receptive to pollen. It is covered commonly with minute papillae, and it is sticky through production of a sugar solution in which the pollen grains germinate.

Stock or rootstock: It is the lower portion of the graft which develops into the root system of the grafted plants.

Style: the tubular upper or middle part of a pistil connecting the stigma and the ovary.

Subclass: A taxon of a rank between class and order.

Subculture: See "passage". With plant cultures this is process by which the tissue or explant is first subdivided, then transferred into fresh culture medium.

Subspecies: A taxon of a rank between species and variety; a group of related varieties.

Substrain: A substrain can be derived from a strain by isolating a single cell or groups of cells having properties or markers not shared by all cells of the parent strain.

Sucker: A rhizome or a branch of a rhizome which comes to the surface and grows into a leafy shoot.

Summer fallow: Allowing land to lie idle for a season to conserve water for use the following season.

Sunburn: A killing of bark near the ground surface due to reflected heat rays, a form of sun scald.

Suspension culture: A type of culture in which cells, or aggregates of cells, multiply while suspended in liquid medium.

Sterility: The inability to set and mature fruit with viable seed. This failure may be due to non-function of the pollen, the ovule or both.

Syconium: An enlarged hollow receptacle bearing flowers and ultimately fruits inside.s

Sympetalous: All the petals coalescent at least basally.

Syncarp: A structure composed of several fruits, these more or less coalescent as for example the fruits of pineapple or mulberry.

Syncarpous: With coalescent carpels.

Syngenesious: With anthers cohering in a circle.

Synsepalous: The sepals coalescent.

Taxon: A category used in classification as for example, a variety, a species, genus, family *etc.* Pural. taxa.

Taxonomy: The principles of classification.

Tepal: A term used for sepals and petals which are similar and not easily distinguished from each other.

Terminal bud: Bud at the end of the stem or a branch.

Testa: The seedcoat, that is, the hardened mature integument.

Tetradynamous: Having four long and two short stamens. A condition found almost throughout the mustard family.

Tetragynous: With four pistils.

Throat: The opening of a sympetalous corolla or a synsepalous calyx, that is, the expanding part between the proper tube and the limb.

Thyrse: A densely congested panicle, the main axis indeterminate, the lateral typically determinate and therefore cymose. A mixed inflorescence.

Tissue: Groups of cells having common functions.

Tissue culture: The term used for range of procedures used to maintain and grow plant tissues and organs in aseptic culture.

Totipotency: A cell characteristic in which the potential for forming all the cell types in the adult organism is retained.

Transpiration: The phenomenon of giving off water in form of vapours.

Tuber: A thickened short underground branch of the stem serving as a storage organ containing reserve food. ex potato.

Umbel: An inflorescence with the pedicles of the flower arising from approximately the same point. A compound umbel is umbal of umbels.

Unfruitful: A plant or variety that fails to set a commercial crop of fruit and mature it.

Unisexual: Of only one sex. Descriptive of a flower having only stamens or only pistils, not both, or of a gymnosperm producing only pollen or only ovules or of the gametophytes of pteridophyte bearing the reproductive organs of only one sex.

Utricle: A small, seeded more or less indehiscent fruit which appears to be inflated, that is, with a relatively thin pericarp more or less remote from the single seed. At maturity the utricle opens either irregularly or along a horizontal line.

Vascular cambium: It is a thin tissue located between the bark (periderm, cortex and phloem) and the wood (xylem).

Vermiculite: It is a micaceous mineral that expands markedly when heated. It is very light in weight, neutral in reaction with good buffering properties and insoluble in water.

Vivipary: The phenomenon in which seeds germinate in the fruit while still attached to the plant.

Water berries: A disorder of the grape in which the fruits are watery and fails to ripen properly.

Wind burn: A disorder of the leaves in which first their edges and later perhaps the entire leaf dries out and present a scorched appearance.

Water spot: A disorder of orange fruits characterized by water soaked appearance.

Xenia: The direct influence of foreign pollen on the part of the mother plant that develops into endosperm.

Xyloporosis: A disorder associated with lack of compatibility between stock and scion, characterized by pores or pits in the wood and corresponding pegs in the bark.

Zygomorphic: Bilaterally symmetrical. Often this is described as irregular, especially with reference to corollas.

Zygote: The fertilized egg, resulting from combining of the male and female gametes.

Bibliography

Abeles, F.B. and Takeda, F. 1990. Cellulase activity and ethylene in ripening strawberry and apple fruits. *Scientia Horticulture*, 42: 269-275.

Biale, J.B. 1960. The postharvest biochemistry of tropical and subtropical fruits. Adv. Food Res. 10: 293-354.

Biale, J.B. 1968. Respiration of fruits. In handbuch der Pflanzenphysiologies, 12: 536-592.

Biale, J.B. and Young, R.E. 1981. Respiration and ripening in fruits – Retrospect and prospect. In: J. Friend and M.J.C. Rhodes (eds.). *Recent Advances in the Biochemistry of Fruits and Vegetables,* Academic Press, London, P. 139.

Chadha, K.L. and Anand, J.C. 1988. Packaging of fresh fruits and vegetables. A Souvenir on packaging of fruits and vegetables in India. *Agri. I horticultural society, public garden, Hyderabad.* Pp. 1-7.

Contractor, J. 1951. The choicest fruit of Hindustan. *Florida mango forum.* Mango studies.

Dilley, D.R. 1972. Postharvest fruit preservation: protein synthesis, ripening and senescence. *Journal of Food Science,* 37(4): 518-520.

El-Zoghbi, M. 1994. Biochemical changes in some tropical fruits during ripening. *Food Chemistry,* 49: 33-37.

Frankel, C., Klein, I. and Dilley, D.R. 1968. "Protein synthesis enzymes in pome fruits". *Plant Physiology,* 1146-1148.

Goodwin, T.W. and Goad, L.J. 1970. Carotenoids and triterpenoids. In: A.C. Hulme (ed.). The biochemistry of fruits and their products. 1: 305-368.

Gortner, W.A., Dull, G.G. and Krauss, B.H. 1967. Fruit development, maturation, ripening and senescence: A biochemical basis for horticultural terminology. *HortScience,* 2: 141-144.

Holl, W. 1977. Fruit ripening. *Plant Research and Development*, 5: 117-126.

Hulme, A.C. 1954. Some aspects of the biochemistry of apple and pear fruits. *Advances in Food Research*, 8: 297-413.

Hulme, A.C. 1958. Study on nitrogen metabolism of apple fruits. The climacteric rise in the respiration in relation to the changes in the equilibrium between protein synthesis and breakdown. *Journal of Experimental Botany*, 5: 159.

Hulme, A.C. 1971. The biochemistry of fruits and their products. Academic Press, London, New York. Vols. I and II.

Iwata, T., Omata, I. and Ogata, K. 1969. Relationship between the ripening of harvested fruits and the respiratory pattern. II. Respiratory pattern of fruits and its classification. *Journal of the Japanese Society of Horticultural Science*, 2: 73-80.

Kader, A.A. 1988. Influence of pre-harvest and postharvest environment on nutritional composition of fruits and vegetables. In: B. Quebedeaux and F.A. Bliss (eds.), Horticulture and human health – Contributions of fruits and vegetables. Prentice-Hall, Englewood Cliffs, N.J., pp. 18-32.

Kader, A.A. and Morris, L.L. 1978. Prompt handling reduces processing-tomato losses. *California Agriculture*, 32(5): 21-22.

Kidd, F. and West, C. 1930. Physiology of fruit. I. Changes in the respiratory activity of apples during their senescence at different temperatures. *Proceedings of Royal Society Biological Sciences*, 106: 93 and Reports of the Food Investigation Board for the years 1922 onwards.

Kliewer, W.M. 1967. Concentration of tartrates, malates, glucose and fructose in the fruits of the genus *Vitis*. *American Journal of Enology and Viticulture*, 18: 87-96.

Kumar, S. and Goswami, A.K. 1985. Phenol content and peroxidise system in developing apple fruits. *Indian Journal of Horticulture*, 42: 184.

Lieberman, M. 1960. Oxidative activity of cytoplasmic particles of apple: electron transfer chain. *Plant Physiology*, 35: 796-801.

Lutz, J.M. and Hardenburg, R.E. 1968. The commercial storage of fruits, vegetables and florist and nursery stocks. USDA Agric. Hand Book No. 66. Washington, D.C.

Mapson, C.W. 1970. "Vitamins in Fruits; Stability of L-Ascorbic Acid in Biochemistry of Fruits and their Products", Pp. 376-387. Academic Press, London.

Mukharjee, P.K. and Srivastava, L.N. 1967. Importance of maturity and marketing of mango fruits (*M. indica* L.). *Int. Symp. Trop. Subtrop. Fruits*, New Delhi.

Naik, K.C. 1949. South India fruits and their culture, *P. Vandhachaney and Co. Madras*.

Pantastico, Er. B. 1975. Postharvest physiology, handling and utilization of tropical fruits and vegetables. The *avi publication co. Inc.* West port, Connecticut.

Payasi, A. and Sanwal, G.G. 2005. Biochemistry of fruit ripening. *Indian Journal of Agricultural Biochemistry*, 18: 51-60.

Reid, M.S. 1995. Ethylene in plant growth, development and senescence. In: P.J. Davies (ed.), Plant hormones, 2nd edition. Kluwer Academic Publishers, Dordrecht, Pp. 486-508.

Ryall, A.L. and Lipton, W.S. 1972. Handling, transportation and storage of fruits and vegetables. *West port, Connecticut. The avi publishing co. Inc.*

Ryall, A.L. and Penther, W.T. 1974. Handling, transportation and storage of fruits and vegetables. West port, Connecticut, *The avi publishing co. Inc.* Vol. II (Fruits and Tree nuts).

Tucker, G.A. 1993. Introduction. In: Seymour, G.B.; Taylor, J.E.; Tucker, G.A. (Eds.). Biochemistry of fruit ripening. Chapman and Hall, Cambridge. Pp. 1-51.

Tucker, G.A. and Grieveson, D. 1987. Fruit ripening. *Plant physiology and Biochemistry,* 12: 265-318.

Wang, C.Y., Conway, W.S., Abott, J.A., Kramer, G.F. and Sams, E.E. 1993. Postharvest infiltration of polyamines and calcium influences ethylene production and texture change in 'Golden Delicious'apple. *Journal of American Society of Horticultural Science,* 118: 801-806.

Watada, A.E., Herner, R.C. Kader, A.A. Romani, R.J. and Staby, G.L. 1984. Terminology for the description of developmental stages of horticultural crops. *HortScience,* 19; 20-21.

Whiting, G.C. 1970. Sugars. In: A.C. Hulme (ed.). The biochemistry of fruits and their products. Academic *Press,* NY, 1: 1-31.

Wills, R.B.M., Graham, D. and Joyee, D. 1998. Postharvest. An introduction to the physiology and handling of fruit, vegetables and ornamentals. *4th Edition. UNSW Press, Sydney.*

Wilson, L.G., Boyette, M.D. and Estes, G.A. 1999. Postharvest handling and cooling of fresh fruits, vegetables and flowers for small farms, leaflets 800-804. North Carolina Cooperative Extension Service pp. 17.

Index

P

R

S

T

U

V